How to access your on-line resources

Kaplan Financial students will have a MyKaplan account and these extra resources will be available to you online. You do not need to register again, as this process was completed when you enrolled. If you are having problems accessing online materials, please ask your course administrator.

If you are not studying with Kaplan and did not purchase your book via a Kaplan website, to unlock your extra online resources please go to www.en-gage.co.uk (even if you have set up an account and registered books previously). You will then need to enter the ISBN number (on the title page and back cover) and the unique pass key number contained in the scratch panel below to gain access.

You will also be required to enter additional information during this process to set up or confirm your account details.

If you purchased through the Kaplan Publishing website you will automatically receive an e-mail invitation to register your details and gain access to your content. If you do not receive the e-mail or book content, please contact Kaplan Publishing.

Your code and information

This code can only be used once for the registration of one book online. This registration and your online content will expire when the final sittings for the examinations covered by this book have taken place. Please allow one hour from the time you submit your book details for us to process your request.

Please scratch the film to access your unique code.

Please be aware that this code is case-sensitive and you will need to include the dashes within the passcode, but not when entering the ISBN.

CIMA 2019 Professional Examinations

Management Level

Subject P2

Advanced Management Accounting

EXAM PRACTICE KIT

British Library Cataloguing-in-Publication Data

A catalogue record for this book is available from the British Library.

Published by:

Kaplan Publishing UK
Unit 2 The Business Centre
Molly Millar's Lane
Wokingham
Berkshire
RG41 2QZ

ISBN: 978-1-83996-248-6

© Kaplan Financial Limited, 2022

Kaplan Publishing's learning materials are designed to help students succeed in their examinations. In certain circumstances, CIMA can make post-exam adjustment to a student's mark or grade to reflect adverse circumstances which may have disadvantaged a student's ability to take an exam or demonstrate their normal level of attainment (see CIMA's Special Consideration policy). However, it should be noted that students will not be eligible for special consideration by CIMA if preparation for or performance in a CIMA exam is affected by any failure by their tuition provider to prepare them properly for the exam for any reason including, but not limited to, staff shortages, building work or a lack of facilities etc.

Similarly, CIMA will not accept applications for special consideration on any of the following grounds:

- failure by a tuition provider to cover the whole syllabus

- failure by the student to cover the whole syllabus, for instance as a result of joining a course part way through

- failure by the student to prepare adequately for the exam, or to use the correct pre-seen material

- errors in the Kaplan Official Study Text, including sample (practice) questions or any other Kaplan content or

- errors in any other study materials (from any other tuition provider or publisher).

CONTENTS

	Page

Section

Quality and accuracy are of the utmost importance to us so if you spot an error in any of our products, please send an email to mykaplanreporting@kaplan.com with full details.

Our Quality Co-ordinator will work with our technical team to verify the error and take action to ensure it is corrected in future editions.

INDEX TO QUESTIONS AND ANSWERS

OBJECTIVE TEST QUESTIONS

EXAM TECHNIQUES

COMPUTER-BASED ASSESSMENT

Golden rules

1   Make sure you have completed the compulsory 15-minute tutorial before you start the test. This tutorial is available through the CIMA website and focusses on the functionality of the exam. You cannot speak to the invigilator once you have started.

2   These exam practice kits give you plenty of exam style questions to practise so make sure you use them to fully prepare.

3   Attempt all questions, there is no negative marking.

4   Double check your answer before you put in the final answer although you can change your response as many times as you like.

5   Not all questions will be multiple choice questions (MCQs) – you may have to fill in missing words or figures.

6   Identify the easy questions first and get some points on the board to build up your confidence.

7   Attempt 'wordy' questions first as these may be quicker than the computation style questions. This will relieve some of the time pressure you will be under during the exam.

8   If you don't know the answer, flag the question and attempt it later. In your final review before the end of the exam try a process of elimination.

9   Work out your answer on the whiteboard provided first if it is easier for you. There is also an onscreen 'scratch pad' on which you can make notes. You are not allowed to take pens, pencils, rulers, pencil cases, phones, paper or notes into the testing room.

SYLLABUS GUIDANCE, LEARNING OBJECTIVES AND VERBS

A   CIMA 2019 PROFESSIONAL QUALIFICATION

Details regarding the content of the CIMA 2019 professional qualification can be located within the CIMA 2019 professional qualification syllabus document.

You can use the following diagram showing the whole structure of your qualification to help you keep track of your progress. Make sure you seek appropriate advice if you are unsure about your progression through the qualification.

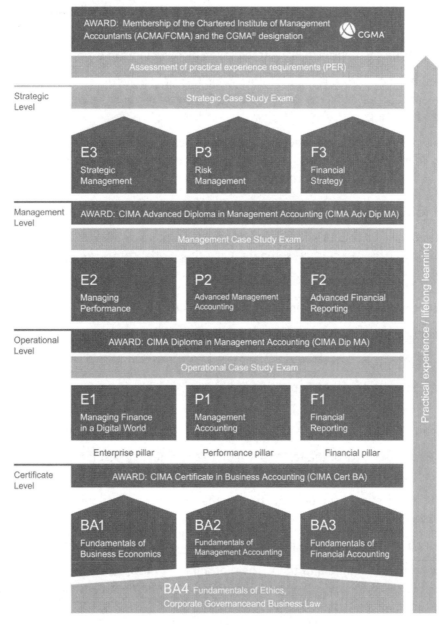

Reproduced with permission from CIMA

B   STUDY WEIGHTINGS

A percentage weighting is shown against each exam content area in the exam blueprint. This is intended as a guide to the proportion of study time each topic requires.

All component learning outcomes will be tested.

The weightings do not specify the number of marks that will be allocated to topics in the examination.

C   LEARNING OUTCOMES

Each subject within the qualification is divided into a number of broad syllabus topics. The topics contain one or more lead learning outcomes, related component learning outcomes and indicative knowledge content.

A learning outcome has two main purposes:

1   to define the skill or ability that a well-prepared candidate should be able to exhibit in the examination

2   to demonstrate the approach likely to be taken by examiners in examination questions.

The learning outcomes are part of a hierarchy of learning objectives. The verbs used at the beginning of each learning outcome relate to a specific learning objective, e.g. Evaluate alternative approaches to budgeting.

The verb 'evaluate' indicates a high-level learning objective. As learning objectives are hierarchical, it is expected that at this level students will have knowledge of different budgeting systems and methodologies and be able to apply them.

The examination blueprints and representative task statements

CIMA have also published examination blueprints giving learners clear expectations regarding what is expected of them. This can be accessed here www.cimaglobal.com/examblueprints

The blueprint is structured as follows:

- Exam content sections (reflecting the syllabus document)

- Lead and component outcomes (reflecting the syllabus document)

- Representative task statements.

A representative task statement is a plain English description of what a CIMA finance professional should know and be able to do.

The content and skill level determine the language and verbs used in the representative task.

CIMA will test up to the level of the task statement in the objective test (an objective test question on a particular topic could be set at a lower level than the task statement in the blueprint).

The format of the objective test blueprints follows that of the published syllabus for the 2019 CIMA Professional Qualification.

Weightings for content sections are also included in the individual subject blueprints.

A list of the learning objectives and the verbs that appear in the syllabus learning outcomes and examinations follows and these will help you to understand the depth and breadth required for a topic and the skill level the topic relates to.

CIMA verb hierarchy

Skill level	Verbs used	Definition
Level 5 Evaluation How you are expected to use your learning to evaluate, make decisions or recommendations	Advise	Counsel, inform or notify
	Assess	Evaluate or estimate the nature, ability or quality of
	Evaluate	Appraise or assess the value of
	Recommend	Propose a course of action
	Review	Assess and evaluate in order, to change if necessary
Level 4 Analysis How you are expected to analyse the detail of what you have learned	Align	Arrange in an orderly way
	Analyse	Examine in detail the structure of
	Communicate	Share or exchange information
	Compare and contrast	Show the similarities and/or differences between
	Develop	Grow and expand a concept
	Discuss	Examine in detail by argument
	Examine	Inspect thoroughly
	Interpret	Translate into intelligible or familiar terms
	Monitor	Observe and check the progress of
	Prioritise	Place in order of priority or sequence for action
	Produce	Create or bring into existence
Level 3 Application How you are expected to apply your knowledge	Apply	Put to practical use
	Calculate	Ascertain or reckon mathematically
	Conduct	Organise and carry out
	Demonstrate	Prove with certainty or exhibit by practical means
	Prepare	Make or get ready for use
	Reconcile	Make or prove consistent/compatible
Level 2 Comprehension What you are expected to understand	Describe	Communicate the key features of
	Distinguish	Highlight the differences between
	Explain	Make clear or intelligible/state the meaning or purpose of
	Identify	Recognise, establish or select after consideration
	Illustrate	Use an example to describe or explain something
Level 1 Knowledge What you are expected to know	List	Make a list of
	State	Express, fully or clearly, the details/facts of
	Define	Give the exact meaning of
	Outline	Give a summary of

D OBJECTIVE TEST

Objective test

Objective test questions require you to choose or provide a response to a question whose correct answer is predetermined.

The most common types of objective test question you will see are:

- Multiple choice, where you have to choose the correct answer(s) from a list of possible answers. This could either be numbers or text.

- Multiple response, for example, choosing two correct answers from a list of eight possible answers. This could either be numbers or text.

- Fill in the blank, where you fill in your answer within the provided space.

- Drag and drop, for example, matching a technical term with the correct definition.

- Hot spots, where you select an answer by clicking on graphs/diagrams.

Guidance re CIMA on-screen calculator

As part of the CIMA objective test software, candidates are now provided with a calculator. This calculator is on-screen and is available for the duration of the assessment. The calculator is available in each of the objective tests and is accessed by clicking the calculator button in the top left hand corner of the screen at any time during the assessment. Candidates are permitted to utilise personal calculators as long as they are an approved CIMA model. CIMA approved model list is found here: https://www.cimaglobal.com/Studying/study-and-resources/.

All candidates must complete a 15-minute exam tutorial before the assessment begins and will have the opportunity to familiarise themselves with the calculator and practise using it. The exam tutorial is also available online via the CIMA website. Candidates can use their own calculators providing it is included in CIMA's authorised calculator listing.

Fundamentals of objective tests

The objective tests are 90-minute assessments comprising 60 compulsory questions, with one or more parts. There will be no choice and all questions should be attempted. All elements of a question must be answered correctly for the question to be marked correctly. All questions are equally weighted.

APPROACH TO REVISION

Stage 1: Assess areas of strengths and weaknesses

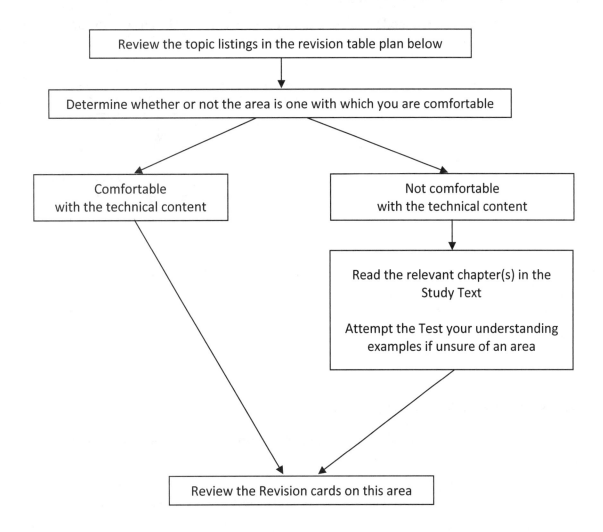

Review the topic listings in the revision table plan below

Determine whether or not the area is one with which you are comfortable

Comfortable
with the technical content

Not comfortable
with the technical content

Read the relevant chapter(s) in the Study Text

Attempt the Test your understanding examples if unsure of an area

Review the Revision cards on this area

Stage 2: Question practice

Follow the order of revision of topics as recommended in the revision table plan below and attempt the questions in the order suggested.

Try to avoid referring to text books and notes and the model answer until you have completed your attempt.

Try to answer the question in the allotted time.

Review your attempt with the model answer and assess how much of the answer you achieved in the allocated exam time.

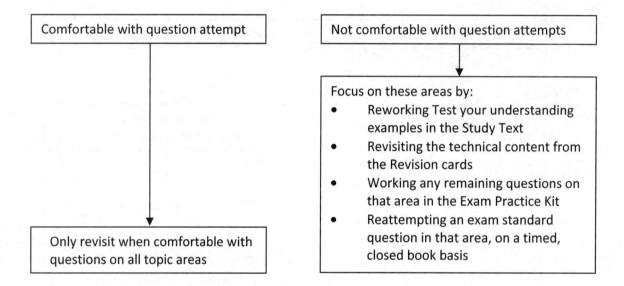

Comfortable with question attempt	Not comfortable with question attempts
	Focus on these areas by: • Reworking Test your understanding examples in the Study Text • Revisiting the technical content from the Revision cards • Working any remaining questions on that area in the Exam Practice Kit • Reattempting an exam standard question in that area, on a timed, closed book basis
Only revisit when comfortable with questions on all topic areas	

Stage 3: Final pre-exam revision

We recommend that you **attempt at least one ninety minute mock examination** containing a set of previously unseen exam standard questions.

It is important that you get a feel for the breadth of coverage of a real exam without advanced knowledge of the topic areas covered – just as you will expect to see on the real exam day.

Ideally a mock examination offered by your tuition provider should be sat in timed, closed book, real exam conditions.

SYLLABUS GRIDS

P2: Advanced Management Accounting

Making medium-term decisions and managing costs and performance

Content weighting

Content area		Weighting
A	Managing the costs of creating value	20%
B	Capital investment decision-making	35%
C	Managing and controlling the performance of organisational units	30%
D	Risk and control	15%
		100%

P2A: Managing the costs of creating value

Cost management and transformation are priorities for organisations facing intense competition. This section examines how to use cost management, quality and process management, and value management to transform the cost structures and drivers to provide organisations with cost advantage.

Lead outcome	Component outcome	Topics to be covered	Explanatory notes
1. Apply cost management and cost transformation methodology to manage costs and improve profitability.	Apply the following to manage costs and improve profitability: a. Activity based management (ABM) methodology b. Cost transformation techniques	• Engendering a cost-conscious culture • Logic of ABC as the foundation or managing costs • ABM to transform efficiency of repetitive overhead activities • ABM to analyse and improve customer profitability • ABM to analyse and improve channel performance	One of the reasons for calculating costs is to enable organisations to manage and possibly transform their costs. ABM is a key technique that is used to achieve this objective because of its link to ABC. This revolves around the logic of ABC that links costs to resource consumption and levels of activity and is related to the business model framework. Customer and channel analysis have become very important in the digital world – particularly as customers shift from products and services to experience. How profitable are the segments and channels they use?
2. Compare and contrast quality management methodologies.	Compare and contrast: a. Just-in-time (JIT) b. Quality management c. Kaizen d. Process re-engineering	• Impact of JIT and quality management on efficiency, inventory and costs • Benefits of JIT and TQM • Kaizen, continuous improvement and cost of quality reporting • Elimination of non-value adding activities and the reduction of costs using process re-engineering	Quality management is an important part of managing and transforming costs. What are the key methodologies? How do they affect the costs of products, services and the channels that are used to deliver them?
3. Apply value management techniques to manage costs and improve value creation.	Apply the following to manage costs and value creation: a. Target costing b. Value chain analysis c. Life cycle costing	• Determination of target costs from target prices • Components of the value chain • Profitability along the value chain • Life cycle costing and its implication for market strategies	Cost transformation must always be linked to the value that organisations create. This part provides the link between costs and value.

P2B: Capital investment decision-making

Organisations have to allocate resources and key strategic initiatives to ensure that their strategies are properly implemented. Capital investment decision-making is the primary means by which such resources are allocated between competing needs. This section covers the criteria, process and techniques that are used to decide which projects to undertake. Of particular interest is the financial appraisal of digital transformation projects.

Lead outcome	Component outcome	Topics to be covered	Explanatory notes
1. Apply the data required for decision-making.	Apply the following for decision-making: a. Relevant cash flows b. Non-financial information	• Incremental cash flows • Tax, inflation and other factors • Perpetuities • Qualitative issues • Sources and integrity of data • Role of business intelligence systems	The quality of decisions depends on the quality and type of data that is available to decision-makers. What type of data do decision-makers need for medium-term decisions? Where do they get this data? In a digital world this would come from data lakes through to data warehouses and business intelligence systems.
2. Explain the steps and pertinent issues in the decision-making process.	Explain: a. Investment decision-making process b. Discounting c. Capital investments as real options	• Origination of proposals, creation of capital budgets, go/no go decisions • Time value of money • Comparing annuities • Profitability index for capital rationing • Decision to make follow-on investment, abandon or wait (capex as real options)	What are the steps in the investment decision-making process for simple as well as complex decisions? What key concepts underpin the techniques that are used? What are the criteria for accepting projects? How is uncertainty dealt with?
3. Apply investment appraisal techniques to evaluate different projects.	Apply the following to evaluate projects: a. Payback b. Accounting rate of return c. IRR d. NPV	• Process and calculation • Strengths and weaknesses • Appropriate usage • Use in prioritisation of mutually exclusive projects	This part covers a straight forward application of the techniques used to appraise projects. These should be extended to deal with the evaluation of digital transformation projects that do not have the same profile as other capital projects.
4. Discuss pricing strategies.	Discuss: a. Pricing decisions b. Pricing strategies	• Pricing decisions for maximising profit in imperfect markets • Types of pricing strategies • Financial consequences of pricing strategies	What pricing strategies are open to organisations operating in imperfect markets? How do these affect the capital investment decision process?

P2C: Managing and controlling the performance of organisational units

The structure and strategies of organisations should align with each other to ensure effective strategy implementation. Responsibility centres are the organisational units that are allocated resources and charged with implementing organisational strategy. This section shows how to manage the performance of these organisational units to ensure that they achieve the strategic and other organisational objectives. Key concepts, techniques and issues are explored and examined.

Lead outcome	Component outcome	Topics to be covered	Explanatory notes
1. Analyse the performance of responsibility centres and prepare reports.	a. Analyse performance of cost centres, revenue centres, profit centres, and investment centres. b. Prepare reports for decision-making.	• Objectives of each responsibility centre • Controllable and uncontrollable costs and revenue • Costs variability, attributable costs and revenue and identification of appropriate measures of performance • Use of data analytics in performance management of responsibility centres	What are responsibility centres and how should they be matched to the strategy of organisations? What are the KPIs of each type of responsibility centre? How is their performance evaluated and why? What types of reports are prepared for responsibility centre managers? How do they use analytics, visualisation and self-service technologies to enhance the performance management of responsibility centres?
2. Discuss various approaches to the performance and control of organisations.	a. Discuss budgets and performance evaluation. b. Discuss other approaches to performance evaluation.	• Key performance indicators (e.g., profitability, liquidity, asset turnover, return on investment and economic value) • Benchmarking (internal and external) • Non-financial performance indicators • Balanced scorecard	How are budgets used to evaluate the performance of responsibility centres? What is best practice in this area? How are other methodologies like the balanced scorecard useful in managing performance?
3. Explain the behavioural and transfer pricing issues related to the management of responsibility centres.	Explain: a. Behavioural issues b. Use and ethics of transfer pricing	• Internal competition • Internal trading • Transfer pricing for intermediate goods where markets exist and where no markets exist • Types of transfer prices and when to use them • Effect of transfer pricing on autonomy, and motivation of managers of responsibility centre • Effect of transfer pricing on responsibility centre and group profitability	What are the behavioural issues in responsibility centre performance management – in particular as they affect controllable and non-controllable costs and revenue? How should they be managed so that responsibility centres work effectively with each other to maximise performance of the whole organisation rather than each responsibility centre? What role can transfer pricing play in this area?

P2D: Risk and control

Risk is inherent in the operations of all organisations. This section analyses risks and uncertainties that organisations face in the medium term. The risks are mainly operational in nature.

Lead outcome	Component outcome	Topics to be covered	Explanatory notes
1. Analyse risk and uncertainty associated with medium-term decision-making.	Conduct a. Sensitivity analysis b. Analysis of risk	• Quantification of risk • Use of probabilistic models to interpret distribution of project outcomes • Stress-testing of projects • Decision trees • Decision-making under uncertainty	What risks do organisations face in relation to capital investment decision-making and the implementation of those decisions? How are those risks incorporated in the decision-making process and managed in the implementation of the decisions?
2. Analyse types of risk in the medium term.	a. Analyse types of risk b. Manage risk	• Upside and downside risks • TARA framework – transfer, avoid, reduce, accept • Business risks • Use of information systems and data in managing risks	

P2D: Risk and control

**Information concerning formulae and tables will be provided via the CIMA website:
www.cimaglobal.com.**

Section 1

OBJECTIVE TEST QUESTIONS

A: MANAGING THE COSTS OF CREATING VALUE

1   EFG has recently introduced an activity-based costing system. It manufactures three products, details of which are set out below:

	Product E	Product F	Product G
Budgeted annual production (units)	75,000	120,000	60,000
Batch size (units)	200	60	30
Machine set-ups per batch	5	3	9
Purchase orders per batch	4	2	2
Processing time per unit (minutes)	3	4	4

Three cost pools have been identified. Their budgeted costs for the year ending 30 September 20X3 are as follows:

Machine set-up costs	$180,000
Purchasing of materials	$95,000
Processing	$110,000

The budgeted machine set-up cost per unit of product F is nearest to:

A $0.17

B $0.35

C $0.76

D $3.10

2   **Which THREE of the following statements regarding the use of Activity Based Costing (ABC) information are correct?**

A   An ABC system produces future information relating to product costs

B   ABC can support decisions regarding changes to the range and mix of products

C   ABC systems are useful for longer-term decisions because all factors of production become variable in the longer term

D   Unlike traditional systems, ABC systems assume that products consume activities in proportion to their production volumes

E   ABC systems remedy the tendency of traditional costing systems to over-cost high-volume products and under-cost low-volume products

3 AB Company is a supermarket group that incurs the following costs:

(i) The bought-in price of the good

(ii) Inventory financing costs

(iii) Shelf refilling costs

(iv) costs of repacking or 'pack out' prior to storage before sale.

AB Company's calculation of direct product profit (DPP) would include:

A All of the above costs

B All of the above costs except (ii)

C All of the above costs except (iv)

D Costs (i) and (iii) only

4 A company sells five products. Sales data for the past year are as follows:

Product	Sales Units	Sales price per unit $
A	2,000	25
B	1,000	40
C	6,000	5
D	5,000	20
E	10,000	2

How would a Pareto analysis of sales revenue be presented, in a table format?

A In the order A, B, C, D, E

B In the order D, A, B, C, E

C In the order E, C, D, A, B

D In the order B, A, D, C, E

5 M manufactures three products: A, B and C. Products A and B are manufactured in batches of ten units. Product C is a high-value product that is manufactured in single units.

In a typical month, production comprises 500 units of A, 400 of B and 20 of C. Product C is manufactured to order and it is very unusual for M to make more than one unit of C per day.

The quality control department has to inspect each unit produced. The department costs a total of $5,020 per month to run.

The monthly cost of running the quality control department is broken down as follows:

	$
Setting up test equipment	2,200
Inspection	2,820

The test equipment has to be set up differently for each product. Once set up, the equipment can test up to ten units before it has to be recalibrated. The time and cost of setting up the equipment is the same for each product.

Each unit of A and B requires the same amount of time for inspection. Each unit of C requires twice as much inspection time. M has an activity-based management system.

The cost per unit of quality control for each unit of C under an activity-based management approach is (in $, two decimal points):

$ [   ]

6   **Kaizen costing emphasises:**

A   the need to achieve a target and maintain it

B   continuous improvement

C   the immediate elimination of all inefficiencies

D   Japanese culture

7   A bakery produces and sells a range of products. The following represents the results for the last month

Product	Contribution
	$000
Brown loaves	67
Family-sized cakes	53
Filled rolls	26
Individual cakes	83
Pasties and pies	16
Plain rolls	42
White loaves	94

Select ALL the statements that apply below:

○   Pasties and Pies are the least profitable product.

○   Four of the product lines make up nearly 80% of the contribution for the bakery firm.

○   The most profitable products are bread and cakes.

○   White loaves outsell all other products, in value terms.

○   Management attention should be focused on bread and cakes, which represent 78% of the profitability of the bakery.

8   **Complete the following text by selecting the missing words and phrases (the same word may be used more than once):**

activities	cost pools	cost	inspections
activity	quality inspection	driver	standards
multiple	single	factor	

A cost _____ is any _____ that causes a change in the _____ of an _____, so the most important factor when selecting a _____ driver is to identify a causal relationship between the cost driver and the costs. Such a relationship may arise because of some physical relationship or because of the logic of the situation.

For example, _____ costs are caused by the action of carrying out an inspection to ensure quality _____ are being achieved, so the appropriate cost _____ would be the number of _____ carried out. Some _____ may have _____ cost drivers associated with them; in such a situation it is best if the costs can be analysed into separate _____ for each of which a _____ driver can be identified.

9 X PLC

X plc manufactures three products in a modern manufacturing plant, using cell operations. Budgeted output for April 2009 was

Product R 1,800 units in 36 batches

Product S 1,000 units in 10 batches

Product T 1,000 units in 40 batches

The product details are as follows:

Product:	R	S	T
Standard labour hours per batch	25	30	15
Batch size (units)	50	100	25
Machine set-ups per batch	3	2	5
Power (kJ) per batch	1.4	1.7	0.8
Purchase orders per batch	5	3	7
Machine hours per batch	10	7.5	12.5

During April 2009, the actual output was

Product R 1,500 units in 30 batches

Product S 1,200 units in 12 batches

Product T 1,000 units in 40 batches

The following production overhead budgetary control statement has been prepared for April 2009 on the basis that the variable production overhead varies in relation to standard labour hours produced.

Production overhead budgetary control report April 2009

Output (standard hours produced)	Original budget	Flexed budget	Actual	Variances
	1,800	1,710	1,710	
	$000	$000	$000	$000
Power	1,250	1,220	1,295	75 (A)
Stores	1,850	1,800	1,915	115 (A)
Maintenance	2,100	2,020	2,100	80 (A)
Machinery cleaning	800	760	870	110 (A)
Indirect labour	1,460	1,387	1,510	123 (A)
	7,460	7,187	7,690	503 (A)

After the above report had been produced, investigations revealed that every one of the individual costs could be classified as wholly variable in relation to the appropriate cost drivers.

Budgeted cost per driver for each of the overhead costs, in $:

Power:

per KJ

Stores:

per order

Maintenance:

per machine hour

Machinery cleaning:

per set-up

10 Having attended a CIMA course on activity-based costing (ABC) you decide to experiment by applying the principles to the four products currently made and sold by your company. Details of the four products and relevant information are given below for one period:

Product	A	B	C	D
Output in units	120	100	80	120
Costs per unit	$	$	$	$
Direct material	40	50	30	60
Direct labour	28	21	14	21
Machine hours (per unit)	4	3	2	3

The four products are similar and are usually produced in production runs of 20 units and sold in batches of 10 units.

The production overhead is currently absorbed by using a machine hour rate, and the total of the production overhead has been analysed as follows:

	$
Machine department costs (rent, business rates, depreciation and supervision)	10,430
Set-up costs	5,250
Stores receiving	3,600
Inspection/quality control	2,100
Material handling and dispatch	4,620

You have ascertained that the 'cost drivers' to be used are as listed below for the overhead costs shown:

Cost	Cost driver
Set-up costs	Number of production runs
Stores receiving	Requisitions raised
Inspection/quality control	Number of production runs
Materials handling and dispatch	Orders executed

The number of requisitions raised on the stores was 20 for each product and the number of orders executed was 42, each order being for a batch of 10 of a product.

If all overhead costs are absorbed on a machine hour basis total costs for each product are:

	Total costs in $
Product A	
Product B	
Product C	
Product D	

If all overhead costs are absorbed using activity based costing, total costs for each product are

	Total costs in $
Product A	
Product B	
Product C	
Product D	

11   Which of the following is not a feature of target costing?

A   Functions of a product are analysed

B   Profit margin on a product is set as a fixed percentage

C   Competitors' products are analysed

D   Selling price of a product is based on its costs

12   In the context of quality costs, customer compensation costs and test equipment running costs would be classified as:

	Customer compensation costs	Test equipment running costs
A	Internal failure costs	Prevention costs
B	Internal failure costs	Appraisal costs
C	External failure costs	Appraisal costs
D	External failure costs	Prevention costs

13   Which of the following are usually elements of a JIT system?

(i)   Machine cells

(ii)   Inventory only held at the bottleneck resource

(iii)   Close relationship with major suppliers

(iv)   Multi-skilled labour

A   (i), (ii) and (iii) only

B   (i), (iii) and (iv) only

C   (i) and (iii) only

D   All of these

14 **Which of the following statements about JIT is correct?**

A   JIT protects an organisation against risks of disruption in the supply chain.

B   A narrow geographical spread in a business makes JIT more difficult to apply.

C   With JIT, there is a risk that inventories could become obsolete.

D   JIT is more difficult to implement when it is not easy to predict patterns of demand.

15 **Which of the following are aspects of a successful JIT system?**

(i)   Demand-driven production.

(ii)   Savings in total machine set-up time.

(iii) Grouping machines or workers by product or component rather than by the type of work performed.

A   (i) and (ii) only

B   (i) and (iii) only

C   (ii) and (iii) only

D   All of these

16 The following details relate to Product Z:

	$/unit
Selling price	45.00
Purchased components	14.00
Labour	10.00
Variable overhead	8.50
Fixed overhead	4.50
Time on bottleneck resource	10 minutes

Product return per minute is:

A $0.80

B $1.25

C $2.10

D $3.10

17   A company manufactures four products – J, K, L and M. The products use a series of different machines but there is a common machine, X, which causes a bottleneck.

The standard selling price and standard cost per unit for each product for the forthcoming year are as follows:

	J	K	L	M
	$	$	$	$
Selling price	2,000	1,500	1,500	1,750
Cost:				
Direct materials	410	200	300	400
Labour	300	200	360	275
Variable overheads	250	200	300	175
Fixed overheads	360	300	210	330
Profit	680	600	330	570
Machine X – minutes per unit	120	100	70	110

Using a throughput accounting approach, the ranking of the products would be:

	J	K	L	M
A	1st	2nd	3rd	4th
B	1st	2nd	4th	3rd
C	2nd	1st	4th	3rd
D	2nd	3rd	1st	4th

18   The selling price of product K is set at $450 for each unit and sales for the coming year are expected to be 600 units.

If the company requires a return of 20% in the coming year on its investment of $300,000 in product K, the target cost for each unit for the coming year is:

A $300

B $350

C $400

D $450

19   A company produces two products, S and T, which pass through two production processes, X and Y. The time taken to make each product in each process is:

	Product S	Product T
Process X	5 mins	7.5 mins
Process Y	18 mins	12 mins

The company operates a 15-hour day and the processes have an average downtime each day of:

Process X	1.5 hours
Process Y	1.0 hours

The costs and revenue for each unit of each product are:

	Product S	Product T
	$	$
Direct materials	20.00	20.00
Direct labour	18.00	14.00
Variable overhead	4.00	4.00
Fixed costs	5.00	4.00
Total cost	48.00	42.00
Selling price	$95.00	$85.00

Sales demand restricts the output of S and T to 50 and 80 units a day respectively.

Calculate the daily production plan that would maximise the throughput contribution.

20   **Indicate, by clicking in the relevant boxes, whether the following statements about a switch to a Just In Time (JIT) inventory control system are true or false.**

Statements	True	False
Throughput contribution per hour is likely to be reduced.		
The differences between marginal and absorption costing profit will be reduced.		

21   **Which of the following statements regarding Total Quality Management (TQM) is not true?**

A   Customer needs are placed above those of the organisation's needs.

B   TQM will often involve the use of Just In Time (JIT) inventory control.

C   TQM believes that the costs of prevention are less than the costs of correction.

D   TQM is a principle that should only be applied to a manufacturing organisation.

22 S Company manufactures accessories for the car industry. The following annual information regarding three of its key customers is available:

	J	H	K
Gross margin	$2,000,000	$3,000,000	$2,500,000
General administration costs	$65,000	$110,000	$52,000
Units sold	20,000	32,000	27,500
Orders placed	1,500	1,500	2,000
Sales visits	156	172	208
Invoices raised	3,000	3,000	4,000

The company uses an activity-based costing system and the analysis of customer-related costs is as follows:

Sales visits	$400 per visit
Order processing	$50 per order placed
Despatch costs	$150 per order placed
Billing and collections raised	$150 per invoice

Using customer profitability analysis, the ranking of the customers would be:

	J	H	K
A	1st	2nd	3rd
B	1st	3rd	2nd
C	2nd	1st	3rd
D	3rd	1st	2nd

23 A company is changing its costing system from traditional absorption costing based on labour hours to an ABC system. It has overheads of $156,000 which are related to taking material deliveries.

The delivery information about each product is given below:

Product	X	Y	Z
Total units required	1,000	2,000	3,000
Delivery size	200	400	1,000

Total labour costs are $360,000 for 45,000 hours. Each unit of each product takes the same number of direct hours.

Assuming that the company uses the number of deliveries as its cost driver, what is the increase or decrease in unit costs for Z arising from the change from AC to ABC?

A $0.50 increase

B $0.50 decrease

C $14.00 increase

D $14.00 decrease

24   MB manufactures a product that requires 3.75 hours per unit of machining time. Machine time is a bottleneck resource, because there are a limited number of machines. There are just seven machines, and each is available for up to 15 hours each day, five days a week.

The product has a selling price of $100 per unit, a direct material cost of $40 per unit, a direct labour cost of $10 per unit and a factory overhead cost of $30 per unit. These costs are based on a weekly production and sales volume of 140 units.

What is the throughput accounting ratio? (2 d.p.)

25   **When building up the cost of a product or service using activity-based costing, which of the following would be used as levels of classification?**

(i)   Facility

(ii)   Product

(iii)   Batch

(iv)   Unit

(v)   Value added

(vi)   Non-value added

A   (i) and (ii) only

B   (ii), (iii) and (iv) only

C   (i), (ii), (iii) and (iv)

D   All of them

26   **Which of the following statements are correct?**

(i)   A cost driver is any factor that causes a change in the cost of an activity.

(ii)   For long-term variable overhead costs, the cost driver will be the volume of activity.

(iii)   Traditional absorption costing tends to under-allocate overhead costs to low-volume products.

A   (i) and (iii) only

B   (ii) and (iii) only

C   (i), (ii) and (iii)

D   (i) only

27 RDE plc uses an activity-based costing system to attribute overhead costs to its three products. The following budgeted data relates to the year to 31 December 2018:

Product	X	Y	Z
Production units (000)	15	25	20
Batch size (000 units)	2.5	5	4

Machine set-up costs are caused by the number of batches of each product and have been estimated to be $600,000 for the year.

Calculate the machine set-up costs that would be attributed to each unit of product Y:

$ [   ]

28 A food processing company operates an activity-based costing (ABC) system.

Which of the following would be classified as a facility-sustaining activity?

(i) General staff administration

(ii) Plant management

(iii) Technical support for individual products and services

(iv) Updating of product specification database

(v) Property management

A (i), (ii) and (v)

B (ii), (iii) and (iv)

C (ii), (iii), (iv) and (v)

D All of them

29 The following data refers to a soft drinks manufacturing company that passes its product through five processes and is currently operating at optimal capacity.

Process	Washing	Filling	Capping	Labelling	Packing
Time per unit	6 mins	3 mins	1.5 mins	2 mins	6 mins
Machine hours available	1,200	700	250	450	1,300

Product data	$ per unit
Selling price	0.60
Direct material	0.18
Direct labour	0.02
Factory fixed cost	$4,120

Calculate:

The maximum output possible in the time available: [   ]

The throughput accounting ratio (2 d.p.): [   ]

30   The following statements have all been claimed to relate to the adoption of a TQM approach. Tick ALL that apply:

○   Employees should focus on the requirements of their customers, both internal and external.

○   Standard costing is unlikely to be used as a method of control.

○   TQM companies often dispense with the quality control department.

31   Which of the following costs are likely to be reduced on the introduction of a JIT system in a company? Tick ALL that apply:

○   Purchasing costs

○   Inventory holding costs

○   Ordering costs

○   Information system costs

32   Which of the following statements relating to JIT and TQM approaches is most closely related to the truth?

A   TQM and JIT are not very compatible approaches since their focus is different: one focuses on quality and the other on inventory levels.

B   TQM and JIT are not usually seen together since TQM is used by service companies and JIT by manufacturing companies.

C   TQM and JIT are very compatible approaches as they are both largely focused on customer satisfaction.

D   TQM and JIT are not compatible approaches since TQM requires there to be inventory so that quality checking can take place.

33   Which of the following is not a term normally used in value analysis?

A   Resale value

B   Use value

C   Esteem value

D   Cost value

34   Which of the following is not suitable for a JIT production system?

A   Batch production

B   Jobbing production

C   Process production

D   Service production

35   Companies that embrace TQM often split their costs into four categories: prevention costs, appraisal costs, internal failure costs and external failure costs. A company wants to categorise the following costs:

(i)   Training staff in the importance of quality.

(ii)   Replacing, from inventory, a defective item returned by a customer.

(iii)   Scrapping an item deliberately tested to destruction.

(iv)   Losses on the sale of items identified as rejects.

Which categories best reflect the nature of the above costs?

	Prevention costs	Appraisal costs	Internal failure costs	External failure costs
A	(i)	(ii)	(iii)	(iv)
B	(i)	(iii)	(iv)	(ii)
C	(ii)	(iv)	(iii)	(i)
D	(iii)	(i)	(iv)	(ii)

36   **Complete the following text by selecting the missing words and phrases (the same word may be used more than once):**

reliability	cost	function	quality
value	quality inspection	driver	economically
relationships	functional	factors	reduction

_____ analysis is an examination of the _____ affecting the cost of a product or service with the objective of achieving the specified purpose most _____ at the required level of _____ and _____.

_____ analysis is an analysis of the _____ between product functions, the _____ of their provision and their perceived _____ to the customer.

Therefore, _____ analysis is a form of cost _____ which is based upon investigating the processes involved in providing a product or service, whereas _____ analysis focuses on the value to the customer of each _____ of the product or service and from this determines whether it is necessary to reduce the cost of providing each function.

37   **Direct Product Profitability is most commonly found in:**

A   The car manufacturing industry

B   The grocery trade

C   Product design departments

D   The travel agency business

E   Production departments

38   **Which of the following is not normally impacted by a move to a Just In Time (JIT) inventory control system?**

  A   The production process

  B   The material requisition process

  C   Staff working hours

  D   The finished goods delivery process

39   **Complete the following text by selecting the missing words and phrases (the same word may be used more than once):**

updated	reduction in stock levels	releases	several
continuous improvement	customer lead	manufacturing	cellular
zero	high	reduction	target

Just-in-Time, like so many modern management techniques, places great importance on the '_____' ethos. Cost containment will often aim to achieve a pre-determined _____, but this _____ may often remain static over a long period of time. With modern techniques, the target is regularly _____ and made more stringent.

Continual cost _____ can be seen in many areas of JIT:

- _____ – large amounts of capital is tied up in _____ stock levels. Reducing stock levels _____ this cash, so that it can be better used elsewhere in the business. Ideally, _____ stock should be held.

- Reduction in _____ times and _____ times – the demand based manufacturing of JIT, together with _____ manufacturing enables production times to be greatly reduced. This will improve customer satisfaction and hopefully lead to increased business volume.

- Cross-training of staff: new production methods necessitate staff being competent in _____ tasks. This may lead to fewer staff being required hence costs are reduced.

40   **Drag and drop the four following labels onto their appropriate definition:**

Prevention costs	Appraisal costs	Internal failure costs	External failure costs

Costs associated with stopping the output of products which fail to conform to the specifications.	Costs of materials or products that fail to meet specifications.
Costs arising when poor quality products are delivered to customers.	Costs associated with ensuring that production meets standards.

41 A company has recently adopted throughput accounting as a performance measuring tool. Its results for the last month are shown below.

Units produced		1,150
Units sold		800
Materials purchased	900 kg costing	$13,000
Opening material inventory used	450 kg costing	$7,250
Labour costs		$6,900
Overheads		$4,650
Sales price		$35

There was no opening inventory of finished goods or closing inventory of materials.

What is the throughput accounting ratio for this product? (2 d.p.)

42 The 'materials handling' business process of Company A consists of the following activities: materials requisitioning, purchases requisitioning, processing purchase orders, inspecting materials, storing materials and paying suppliers. This process could be re-engineered by sending the materials requisitions directly to an approved supplier, and entering into an agreement which entails delivering high quality materials in accordance with production requirements.

Which of the following cost reductions would be expected after re-engineering the materials handling process? Select ALL that apply.

(i) Cost reduction due to the elimination of the administration involved in placing orders.

(ii) Cost reduction due to the elimination of the need for material inspection.

(iii) Cost reduction due to the elimination of the need for material storage.

A (i) only

B (i) and (ii) only

C (ii) and (iii) only

D All of them

43 **What attempts to move away from a traditional hierarchic organisation structure, in order to respond to the demands of a customer service-oriented business environment, where quality is the key strategic variable?**

A Business Process Re-engineering

B Total Quality Management

C Continuous Process Improvement

D Business Process Management

44   Complete the following text by selecting the missing words and phrases (the same word may be used more than once):

internal	sequence	relationships	quality
value	customers	distribution	value chain
products	suppliers	factors	chain

The extended value _____ includes both _____ and external _____ whereas the _____ includes only the internal factors. The value chain is the _____ of business _____ that add _____ to the organisation's _____ and services and comprises the following:

- Research and Development (R&D)

- Design

- Production

- Marketing

- _____

- Customer service

The extended value chain adds _____ to the left hand side and _____ to the right hand side and recognises the importance of the _____ that the organisation has with these external parties in the overall process of adding value.

45   Konta Ltd has produced the following estimates for a new product with an expected life of three years:

	Year 1	Year 2	Year 3
Units made and sold	3,000	6,000	5,000
	$	$	$
Design costs	2,000	500	500
Variable production cost per unit	15.20	14.80	14.50
Fixed production costs	2,700	2,800	2,900
Variable selling cost per unit	0.80	0.90	0.95
Distribution and customer service costs	2,000	3,500	2,500

What is the life-cycle cost per unit of the new product?

A $15.59

B $16.85

C $17.06

D $17.23

46   **In calculating the life cycle costs of a product, which of the following items would be excluded?**

   (i)   Planning and concept design costs

   (ii)   Preliminary and detailed design costs

   (iii)   Testing costs

   (iv)   Production costs

   (v)   Distribution and customer service costs

   A   (iii)

   B   (iv)

   C   (v)

   D   None of them

B: CAPITAL INVESTMENT DECISION-MAKING

47   **X PLC**

X plc intends to use relevant costs as the basis of the selling price for a special order: the printing of a brochure. The brochure requires a particular type of paper that is not regularly used by X plc although a limited amount is in X plc's inventory which was left over from a previous job.

The cost when X plc bought this paper last year was $15 per ream and there are 100 reams in inventory. The brochure requires 250 reams. The current market price of the paper is $26 per ream, and the resale value of the paper in inventory is $10 per ream.

What is the relevant cost of the paper to be used in printing the brochure?

$ [   ]

48   T plc manufactures a component D12, and two main products F45 and P67. The following details relate to each of these items:

	D12	F45	P67
	$ per unit	$ per unit	$ per unit
Selling price	–	146.00	159.00
Material cost	10.00	15.00	26.00
Component D12 (bought-in price)	–	25.00	25.00
Direct labour	5.00	10.00	15.00
Variable overheads	6.00	12.00	18.00
Total variable cost per unit	21.00	62.00	84.00

Fixed overhead costs:	$ per annum	$ per annum	$ per annum
Avoidable*	9,000	18,000	40,000
Non-avoidable	36,000	72,000	160,000
Total	45,000	90,000	200,000

* The avoidable fixed costs are product-specific fixed costs that would be avoided if the product or component were to be discontinued.

Assuming that the annual demand for component D12 is 5,000 units and that T plc has sufficient capacity to make the component itself, what is the maximum price that should be paid to an external supplier for 5,000 components per year?

Assuming that component D12 is bought from an external supplier for $25.00 per unit, what number of units of product F45 that must be sold to cover its own costs without contributing to T plc's non-avoidable fixed costs?

49   You are currently in employment earning $25,000 per annum. You have decided to go into business for yourself doing PC repairs for local companies and will operate out of a unit available for rent at the edge of the town.

How should (i) your current salary and (ii) the rent of the unit be treated when deciding whether or not to start the business?

A   (i) as an irrelevant cost and (ii) as an opportunity cost

B   (i) as a sunk cost and (ii) as an committed cost

C   (i) as an incremental cost and (ii) as an opportunity cost

D   (i) as a committed cost and (ii) as a sunk cost

E   (i) as an opportunity cost and (ii) as an incremental cost

50   **RIGHTLIGHT LTD**

Rightlight Ltd is an advertising company and has been asked to tender for a contract to increase public awareness of global environmental issues as part of the government's commitment to improving the country's eco-footprint.

Rightlight Ltd believes that the campaign work will take a period of six months.

Five advertising specialists would need to be recruited on an annual salary of $45,000. A project manager would be needed to coordinate the campaign. An existing project manager would be used whose annual salary is currently $55,000. They would be expected to devote 30% of their time on the new contract.

The new employees would have to go through a 'Environmental Awareness' training programme in order to get approval to work on government contracts. This would cost $3,000 per employee, but it is anticipated that a grant of 20% towards this cost will be available.

Alternatively, Rightlight Ltd could subcontract the work (with the government's agreement) to another PR that it sometimes uses for joint venture projects. It is anticipated that the subcontract firm would demand a fee of $135,000 to undertake the work.

What would be the relevant cost of labour for this contract?

$ [   ]

51 Indicate, by clicking in the relevant boxes, whether the following are examples of a quantitative cost, a quantitative benefit, a qualitative cost, or a qualitative benefit.

Cost or benefit	Quantitative cost	Quantitative benefit	Qualitative cost	Qualitative benefit
The impact on employee morale of adding a common room with tea and coffee facilities in the production area				
Reduction in sales teams travelling expenses after moving all account management activities to Internet-based support solutions				
Increase in market share				
Lower employee morale and productivity linked to pay cuts				
More recognised corporate branding				
The impact on the community of allowing employees to spend a few hours of paid time assisting local charities				
Advertising investment in e-commerce sites and social media platforms				

52 The details of an investment project are as follows:

Cost of asset bought at the start of the project	$80,000
Annual cash inflow	$25,000
Cost of capital, after tax	5% each year
Life of the project	8 years

Corporation tax is 25% and is paid in equal quarterly instalments in the 6th and 9th months of the year in which the profit was earned and in the 1st and 3rd months of the following year.

Writing down allowances of 20% reducing balance will be claimed each year.

(Assume the asset is bought on the first day of the tax year and that the company's other projects generate healthy profits.)

The present value of the cash flows that occur in the second year of the project is:

A $17,006

B $19,053

C $20,271

D $25,940

53 **Which THREE of the following statements explain the time value of money?**

    A   Machinery tends to deteriorate over time leading to increased operating costs

    B   Future payments are less certain as they may be prevented

    C   Funds lose purchasing power over time

    D   Reported annual profits are subjective because they are affected by accounting policies

    E   There is an investor preference for immediate consumption

54 A company is considering investing in a project that would have a four-year life span. The investment would involve an immediate cash outflow of $250,000 and have a zero residual value. In each of the four years, 6,000 units would be produced and sold. The contribution per unit, based on current prices, is $12. The company has an annual cost of capital of 10%. It is expected that the inflation rate will be 4% in each of the next four years.

The net present value of the project (to the nearest $100) is:

    A $800

    B $1,300

    C $1,800

    D $2,300

55 B Company is deciding whether to launch a new product. The initial outlay for the product is $60,000. The forecast possible annual cash inflows and their associated probabilities are shown below:

	Probability	Year 1	Year 2	Year 3
Optimistic	0.25	$35,000	$40,000	$32,000
Most likely	0.55	$20,000	$26,000	$28,000
Pessimistic	0.20	$18,000	$24,000	$22,000

The company's cost of capital is 8% per annum.

Assume the cash inflows are received at the end of the year and that the cash inflows for each year are independent.

The expected net present value for the product is:

    A   ($500)

    B $8,634

    C $10,189

    D $12,348

56   A company is considering investing in a manufacturing project that would have a three-year life span. The investment would involve an immediate cash outflow of $50,000 and have a zero residual value. In each of the three years, 4,000 units would be produced and sold. The contribution per unit, based on current prices, is $5. The company has an annual cost of capital of 8%. It is expected that the inflation rate will be 3% in each of the next three years.

The net present value of the project (to the nearest $500) is:

A $4,500

B $5,000

C $5,500

D $6,000

57   JAH Company is about to invest $400,000 in machinery and other capital equipment for a new product venture. Cash flows for the first three years are estimated as follows:

Year	$000
1	210
2	240
3	320

JAH Company requires a 17% return for projects of this type. The above cash flows do not include expenditure on an advertising campaign, which will be incurred in equal annual amounts at the beginning of years 1, 2 and 3.

Ignoring any residual values of the capital equipment, calculate the maximum annual amount that can be spent on advertising, to the nearest $000.

$ ☐

58   X Company takes on a five-year lease of a building for which it pays $27,200 as a lump sum payment. X Company then sub-lets the building for five years at a fixed annual rent, with the rent payable annually in arrears.

Calculate (to the nearest $) the annual rental charge, if the rent is set at a level that will earn a DCF yield of 17% for X Company.

$ ☐

59 A company is evaluating a new product proposal. The proposed product selling price is $180 per unit and the variable costs are $60 per unit. The incremental cash fixed costs for the product will be $160,000 per annum. The discounted cash flow calculation results in a positive NPV:

		Cash flow $	Discount rate	Present value $
Year 0	Initial outlay	(1,000,000)	1.000	(1,000,000)
Years 1–5	Annual cash flow	320,000	3.791	1,213,120
Year 5	Working capital released	50,000	0.621	31,050
Net present value				244,170

What is the percentage change in selling price (to 1 d.p.) that would result in the project having a net present value of zero?

[ ] %

60 A company is considering investing in a project that requires an initial outflow of $500,000 and will generate expected cash inflows in terms of today's $ of $130,000 over each of the next four years. The company's monetary cost of capital is 7% and inflation is predicted to be 4% over the next four years.

Calculate:

The company's real cost of capital (2 d.p.)

[ ] %

The net present value of the project, when discounting money cash flow at the money rate:

$ [ ]

The net present value of the project, when discounting real cash flow at the real rate:

$ [ ]

61 **If the money discount rate is 12% and the real rate is 6%, what is the rate of inflation?**

A 5.66%

B 6.30%

C 18.60%

D 17.66%

62   The details of an investment project are:

Life of the project	10 years
Cost of asset bought at the start of the project	$100,000
Annual cash inflow	$20,000
Cost of capital, after tax	8% each year

Corporation tax is 30% and is paid in equal quarterly instalments in the 7th and 10th months of the year in which the profit was earned and in the 1st and 4th months of the following year.

Writing down allowances of 25% reducing balance will be claimed each year.

(Assume the asset is bought on the first day of the tax year and that the company's other projects generate healthy profits. Round all cash flows to the nearest $ and discount end of year cash flows.)

Calculate the present value of the cash flows that occur in the second year of the project:

$ [   ]

63   An investment project that requires an initial investment of $500,000 has a residual value of $130,000 at the end of five years. The project's cash flows have been discounted at the company's cost of capital of 12% and the resulting net present value is $140,500.

The profitability index of the project is closest to:

A   0.02

B   0.54

C   0.28

D   0.26

64   CC Company is considering an investment of $300,000 which will earn a contribution of $40,000 each year for 10 years at today's prices. The contribution will rise at the rate of 6% per year because of inflation. The company's cost of money is 11% per annum.

The net present value of the project is

$ [   ]

65   A company has determined that the net present value of an investment project is $12,304 when using a 10% discount rate and $(3,216) when using a discount rate of 15%.

The internal rate of return of the project, to the nearest 1%, is

[   ] %

66 An investment project with no residual value has a net present value of $87,980 when it is discounted using a cost of capital of 10%. The annual cash flows are as follows:

Year	$
0	(200,000)
1	80,000
2	90,000
3	100,000
4	60,000
5	40,000

Using discount rates of 10% and 20%, calculate the Internal Rate of Return (IRR) of the project (no d.p.):

$ [   ]

67 A company is to spend $60,000 on a machine that will have an economic life of ten years, and no residual value. Depreciation is to be charged using the straight-line method. Estimated operating cash flows are:

Year	$
1	−2,000
2	13,000
3	20,000
4–6	25,000 each year
7–10	30,000 each year

What is the average accounting of return (ARR), calculated as average annual profits divided by the average investment?

A 75%

B 55%

C 38%

D 28%

68 The following statements have been made about the disadvantages of using the Accounting Rate of Return (ARR) method of project appraisal.

Which ONE of these statements is NOT a valid criticism?

A The ARR produced for a project will vary depending on the extent to which costs are capitalised

B ARR does not provide a definite investment signal

C ARR does not take account of the length of a project's life

D ARR has no relationship with other measures used to assess business success

69   **For a company with the objective of maximising net present value, what is the validity of the following statements for a conventional investment project?**

(i)   The accounting rate of return (ARR) method of project appraisal usually gives too little weight to cash flows which occur late in the project's life.

(ii)   For a project with a (unique) IRR greater than the opportunity cost of capital, the IRR method of project appraisal usually gives too little weight to cash flows which occur late in the project's life.

	Statement 1	Statement 2
A	True	True
B	True	False
C	False	False
D	False	True

70   M plc is evaluating three possible investment projects and uses a 10% discount rate to determine their net present values.

Investment	A	B	C
	$000	$000	$000
Initial investment	400	450	350
Incremental cash flows			
Year 1	100	130	50
Year 2	120	130	110
Year 3	140	130	130
Year 4	120	130	150
Year 5*	100	130	100
Net present value	39	55	48

* Includes $20,000 residual value for each investment project.

Calculate the payback period of investment A:

Calculate the discounted payback period of investment B:

Calculate the Internal Rate of Return (IRR) of investment C:

71 X is considering the following five investments:

Investment	J	K	L	M	N
	$000	$000	$000	$000	$000
Initial investment	400	350	450	500	600
Net present value	125	105	140	160	190

Investments J and L are mutually exclusive; all of the investments are divisible and none of them may be invested in more than once.

The optimum investment plan for X assuming that the funding available is limited to $1m is:

A $400,000 in J plus $600,000 in N

B $400,000 in M plus $600,000 in N

C $500,000 in M plus $500,000 in N

D $350,000 in K plus $600,000 in N plus $50,000 in M

72 X ltd can choose from five mutually exclusive projects. The projects will each last for one year only, and their net cash inflows will be determined by the prevailing market conditions. The forecast annual cash inflows and their associated possibilities are shown below:

Market conditions	Poor	Good	Excellent
Probability	0.20	0.50	0.30
	$000	$000	$000
Project L	500	470	550
Project M	400	550	570
Project N	450	400	475
Project O	360	400	420
Project P	600	500	425

Based on the expected value of the cash inflows, which project should be undertaken?

A   L

B   M

C   N

D   O

E   P

73 A company is considering an investment of $400,000 in new machinery. The machinery is expected to yield incremental profits over the next five years as follows:

Year	Profit ($)
1	175,000
2	225,000
3	340,000
4	165,000
5	125,000

Thereafter, no incremental profits are expected and the machinery will be sold. It is company policy to depreciate machinery on a straight line basis over the life of the asset. The machinery is expected to have a value of $50,000 at the end of year 5.

Calculate the payback period of the investment in this machinery to the nearest 0.1 years.

74 The payback period can be used to provide a measure of the risk associated with a project.

Which ONE of the following statements correctly explains the relationship between the payback period of a project and its risk?

A   The shorter the payback of a project, the higher the expected value of the cash flows over the project's life

B   The shorter the payback of a project, the quicker an investor can recover the initial investment and reinvest it elsewhere

C   The shorter the payback period of a project, the higher its liquidity ratio

D   The shorter the payback period of a project, the lower the standard deviation of its predicted cash flows

75 An investment company is considering the purchase of a commercial building at a cost of $0.85m. The property would be rented immediately to tenants at an annual rent of $80,000 payable in arrears in perpetuity.

What is the net present value of the investment, assuming that the investment company's cost of capital is 8% per annum?

Ignore taxation and inflation.

$ [   ]

76   HURON

Huron Ltd wishes to expand its operations. Six possible capital investments have been identified, but Huron only has access to a total of $570,000. The projects have unequal lives, are not divisible and may not be postponed. The following information is available (all calculations are correct and the cash outlays are given in $000):

Project	Outlay in Year	NPV	Profitability Index
A	(246)	$6,350	0.026
B	(180)	$1,882	0.010
C	(175)	$(2,596)	–0.015
D	(180)	$8,294	0.046
E	(180)	$5,490	0.031
F	(150)	$4,993	0.033

Projects A and E are mutually exclusive. All projects are believed to be of similar risk to the company's existing capital investments.

Which combination of projects should be selected?

A   D, E and F

B   A, B and F

C   A, D and F

D   A, D and E

77   **Which TWO of the following situations would limit the use of replacement analysis to determine the most suitable replacement cycle for a specific machine?**

A   Owing to deterioration, repair and maintenance costs tend to be higher the older the machine gets

B   Price inflation has slowed to less than 1% over the past few years

C   Technological advances in the industry are commonplace

D   Investment incentives for new machinery have wiped out the resale market for old equipment

E   Economic forecasts are often inaccurate

78   A machine costs $20,000. The following information is also available:

Running costs (payable at the end of the year) amount to $5,000 at the end of year 1. If the machine was kept on for another year, running costs would amount to $5,500 at the end of that year.

If the machine was disposed of after 1 year, the trade-in allowance would amount to $16,000. For a disposal after 2 years, the trade-in allowance would amount to $13,000.

Calculate the optimal replacement cycle if the cost of capital is 10%. The machine should be replaced after ......

year(s)

79   **A decision has to be made on replacement policy for vans. A van costs $12,000, and the following additional information applies:**

Van is sold at the end of year...	Trade-in allowance	Van kept in business for....	Maintenance cost at the end of the year
1	$9,000	1 year	$0
2	$7,500	2 years	$1,500 in the first year
3	$7,000	3 years	$2,700 in the second year

The cost of capital is 15%. Vans are only maintained at the end of the year if they are to be kept for a further year, i.e. there are no maintenance costs in the year of replacement.

Ignore taxation and inflation. Calculate the optimal replacement policy. Each van should be replaced after......

year(s)

80   A machine costing $150,000 has a useful life of eight years, after which time its estimated resale value will be $30,000. Annual running costs will be $6,000 for the first three years of use and $8,000 for each of the next five years. All running costs are payable on the last days of the year to which they relate.

Using a discount rate of 20% per annum, what is the equivalent annual cost (to the nearest $100) of using the machine, if it were bought and replaced every eight years in perpetuity?

A $21,100

B $34,000

C $30,400

D $44,200

81   The management of a bottling plant are planning to replace one of the main pieces of processing equipment, which will be needed for the foreseeable future. Three different machines have been identified as potential replacements. The machines are expected to last for two, three and four years respectively before they would themselves need to be replaced.

Which of the following methods of selecting between the machines would be the MOST suitable?

A   Choose the machine with the highest discounted payback index

B   Choose the machine with the lowest equivalent annual cost

C   Choose the machine with the highest profitability index

D   Choose the machine with the lowest NPV of costs

82   Pumpkin Ltd is considering purchasing a new machine at a cost of $110,400 that will be operated for four years, after which time it will be sold for an estimated $9,600. Pumpkin uses a straight line depreciation policy. Forecast operating profits to be generated by the machine are as follows:

Year	$
1	39,600
2	19,600
3	22,400
4	32,400

What is the payback period ('PP') and the average accounting rate of return (ARR), calculated as average annual profits divided by the average investment?

A   PP: 2.01 years ARR: 47.5%

B   PP: 3.89 years ARR: 25.8%

C   PP: 3.89 years ARR: 47.5%

D   PP: 2.01 years ARR: 25.8%

83 A company is currently evaluating a project which requires investments of $12,000 now, and $4,800 at the end of year 1. the cash inflow from the project will be $16,800 at the end of year 2 and $14,400 at the end of year 3. The cost of capital is 15%.

Select the discounted payback period (DPP) and the net present value (NPV).

A   DPP: 2.00 years NPV: $6,000

B   DPP: 2.36 years NPV: $4,440

C   DPP: 2.00 years NPV: $4,440

D   DPP: 2.36 years NPV: $6,000

84 The IRR of a project, consisting of an initial outflow followed by several years of inflows, has been calculated to be greater than the company's cost of capital.

The company has therefore decided to accept the project.

Which of the following statements best explains the company's decision?

A   If the project is undertaken, shareholders' wealth will be maintained at a constant level.

B   The project will pay back the initial investment faster than if the money was invested at the company's cost of capital

C   The project is expected to earn a profit

D   The project is expected to earn a rate of return higher than the company's target rate

85 **What does the real required rate of return of a company represent?**

A   The return the company must earn stated in today's prices

B   The company's cost of capital adjusted to include the impact of inflation

C   The company's cost of capital adjusted to include the impact of risk

D   The return the company must earn restated to reflect prices in each of the years in which it will be applied

86 A company has used the following calculation to appraise a capital investment project:

$$\frac{\text{Annual cash inflow}}{\text{Initial investment}}$$

What appraisal technique is the company using?

A   IRR

B   ARR

C   Payback period

D   Modified IRR

87 Which of the following is not an advantage of the IRR?

A It considers the whole life of a project

B It uses cash flows not profits

C It is a measure of absolute return

D It considers the time value of money

88 A management accountant has decided to use the Modified Internal Rate of Return (MIRR) rather than the standard Internal Rate of Return (IRR) to appraise a potential investment and has made the following statements to explain why MIRR is superior to IRR.

Which TWO of the statements are correct?

A There is only one MIRR for a project

B MIRR can be used to replace NPV as the principle evaluation technique

C MIRR provides a measure of return from a project

D MIRR provides a measure of liquidity and risk

E MIRR allows for a decision to be made without reference to the company's cost of capital

89 **Which ONE of the following does NOT apply to the Modified Rate of Return method?**

O The MIRR measures the economic yield of an investment under the assumption that any cash surpluses are reinvested to earn a return equal to the IRR of the original project.

O The MIRR gives a measure of the return from the project, whereas the IRR only represents the return from the project if funds can be re-invested at the IRR for the duration of the project.

O The MIRR gives an indication of the maximum cost of finance that the firm could sustain to allow the project to remain worthwhile.

O The MIRR overcomes the problem of the reinvestment assumption and the fact that changes in the cost of capital over the life of the project cannot be incorporated in the IRR approach.

90 **ONTARIO**

Ontario Ltd's cost of capital is 7% per annum. A project with the following cash flows is under consideration:

T_0	T_1	T_2	T_3	T_4
($22,500)	$7,500	$7,500	$7,400	$7,300

The MIRR for the project is closest to:

A 7%

B 8%

C 9%

D 10%

91   Michigan Ltd's cost of capital is 9% per annum. A project with the following cash flows is under consideration:

T_0	T_1	T_2	T_3	T_4
($67,000)	$20,000	$19,500	$19,000	$19,000

The MIRR for the project is closest to:

A   7%

B   8%

C   9%

D   10%

92   Superior Ltd's cost of capital is 6% per annum. A project with the following cash flows is under consideration:

T_0	T_1	T_2	T_3	T_4
($120,000)	$45,000	$35,000	$35,000	$30,000

The MIRR for the project is closest to:

A   7%

B   8%

C   9%

D   10%

93   When compared with the NPV method, the IRR method has a number of disadvantages.

What is the validity of the following statements?

(i)   The internal rate of return (IRR) ignores the relative size of investments.

(ii)   For a project with non-conventional cash flows, the use of the IRR method can prove problematic or misleading.

	Statement 1	Statement 2
A	True	True
B	True	False
C	False	False
D	False	True

94 A company with a 10% cost of capital uses NPV to evaluate potential projects. All projects consist of an investment followed by several years of cash inflows.

It has appraised one project (Project A) and found that the NPV is $0 at 10% and $4,000 at 8%.

It is also considering a second project (Project B) which has an NPV of $8,000 at 10% and an NPV of $4,000 at 12%.

Which ONE of the following actions should the company take?

A   The company should reject Project A in favour of Project B because Project B has a higher IRR

B   Regardless of Project B, the company should reject Project A as it will not increase shareholder wealth

C   The company should reject Project A in favour of Project B because Project B has a higher NPV at the company's cost of capital

D   Regardless of Project B, the company should accept Project A as it earns their required return

95 The following information relates to a management consultancy:

Wage cost per consultant hour (senior consultant)	$45.00
Wage cost per consultant hour (junior consultant)	$26.00
Overhead absorption rate per consultant hour	$20.50

The firm adds a 25% mark-up on marginal cost to arrive at the price to charge clients.

For client 'Greenstart' 75 hours of senior consultant time and 30 hours of junior consultant time have been incurred. All staff are paid on an hourly basis.

What price should be charged to Greenstart? (2 d.p.)

$ [   ]

96 When deciding upon the price of a product, which of the following items would not be taken into consideration?

Select ALL that apply:

○   Cost of making the product.

○   Price elasticity of demand.

○   Cost of making other unrelated products.

○   Prices charged by competitors serving the same market segments.

○   Level of customer disposable wealth.

97 **When is market skimming pricing appropriate?**

A   If demand is very elastic

B   If the product is new and different

C   If there is little chance of achieving economies of scale

D   If demand is inelastic

E   If there is little competition and high barriers to entry

98 **Which of the following is a recognised method of arriving at the selling price for the products of a business?**

(i)   Life cycle pricing

(ii)   Price skimming

(iii)   Penetration pricing

(iv)   Target costing

A   (i) and (ii) only

B   (i), (ii) and (iii) only

C   (ii) and (iii) only

D   (i), (iii) and (iv) only

E   (i), (ii), (iii) and (iv)

99 **Which of the following circumstances favour a penetration pricing policy?**

(i)   There are significant economies of scale from high volume output

(ii)   Demand is relatively inelastic

(iii)   The firm wishes to discourage new entrants to the market

(iv)   The product life cycle is relatively short

A   (i) and (iii) only

B   (ii) and (iv) only

C   (i), (ii) and (iii) only

D   (ii) and (iii)

E   (i) and (iv)

100 **MALTOV**

Maltov has established the following cost and revenue functions for the single product that it manufactures:

Price = $120 – 0.5 × quantity

Marginal revenue = $120 – 1 × quantity

Total cost = $250,000 + 20 × quantity

The price should Maltov charge for its product in order to maximise profit is:

$ [   ]

101 A factory's entire machine capacity is used to produce essential components. The costs of using the machines are as follows:

Variable costs $15,000

Fixed costs $50,000

Total $65,000

If all the components are purchased from an outside supplier, the machines could be used to produce other items which would earn a total contribution of $25,000.

What is the maximum price that a profit- maximising company should be willing to pay to the outside supplier for the components?

    A $15,000

    B $25,000

    C $40,000

    D $65,000

102 The trust in charge of national landmarks offers discounted entry to visitors with a valid student identity card.

This price discrimination policy is on the basis of:

    A   Place

    B   Usage

    C   Market segment

    D   Time

    E   Product type

103 H is launching a new product which it expects to incur a variable cost of $14 per unit. The company has completed some market research to try to determine the optimum selling price with the following results.

If the price charged was to be $25 per unit then the demand would be 1,000 units each period. For every $1 increase in the selling price, demand would reduce by 100 units each period. For every $1 reduction in the selling price, the demand would increase by 100 units each period.

Calculate:

The selling price per unit needed to maximise profit:

$ [ ]

104 Market research by company a has revealed that the maximum demand for product R is 50,000 units each year and that demand will reduce by 50 units for every $1 that the selling price is increased.

Based on this information, company A has calculated that the profit-maximising level of sales for product R for the coming year is 35,000 units.

The selling price of each of the units at the profit-maximising level of sales is:

$ [ ]

105 SAMSINGING LTD

'Samsinging Ltd' is about to launch a new product to the UK market, the new product is called the 'Songtime'. Sales demand has been estimated based on product launches in a range of similar countries and the expected demand is to be between a low of 50,000 units per month and a high of 400,000 units per month depending upon the price ultimately charged.

The marketing department believe that 50,000 units would be sold if the price is set at $400 per unit. They have also advised that for every decrease in price of $12.50 per unit, an additional 25,000 units would be sold.

Fixed costs are expected to be $48 million per annum if the company produces 250,000 units or less. However, if the level of production exceeds 250,000 units, annual fixed costs are expected to increase by $6 million.

If 250,000 units or less are made, the variable production cost per unit is expected to be $240 per unit. If more than 250,000 units are made, the variable production cost per unit is expected to be $210 per unit. Variable selling cost per unit is expected to be $35 per unit if 150,000 units or less are sold, and $40 per unit if more than 150,000 units are sold.

Produce a table but consider only production and sales levels of 50,000 units, 100,000 units, 150,000 units, 200,000 units, 250,000 units, 300,000 units, 350,000 units and 400,000 units.

What price should be set, given that the primary objective is to maximise profit?

$ _____

106 STALY PLC

Staly plc has two wholly owned UK-based subsidiaries. One of these subsidiaries, Brompton Ltd, manufactures plastic toys which it sells to toy retailers. Brompton Ltd is about to launch a new product but is unsure what price to charge. A firm of consultants have estimated the level of demand at several different prices. This information is as follows:

Price ($)	5	10	15	20	25	30	35	40
Level of demand in forthcoming year (000 of units)	200	180	160	135	120	100	75	50

The cost of manufacturing the new toy has been estimated as follows:

	$ per unit
Direct materials	2.00
Direct labour	1.50
Variable overheads	2.50
	6.00

Fixed costs associated with manufacturing the new toy are expected to be $400,000 per annum. However, if production and sales exceed 150,000 units fixed costs are expected to increase by $50,000.

The second subsidiary, Electrics Ltd, assembles desktop computers using components sourced from suppliers of keyboards, microchips, monitors, speakers and so on. It sells these computers under its own brand name through 150 of its own outlets in major shopping centres throughout the UK.

It is to commence selling a new computer aimed at students. The management of Electrics Ltd believe that the price and marginal revenue equations are as follows:

Price equation:

$P = 2,000 - 0.01Q$

where P is selling price and Q is sales quantity in units.

Marginal revenue (MR) equation:

$MR = 2,000 - 0.02Q$

The cost of manufacture is expected to be:

	$ per unit
Direct materials (bought-in components)	400
Direct labour (assembly)	150
Variable overheads	50
Fixed overheads (apportioned)	200
	800

For Brompton Ltd, what price should be set for the new toy in order to maximise profit?

$ [_____]

What price should be set to maximise profit for Electrics Ltd?

$ [_____]

What price should be set to maximise revenue for Electrics Ltd?

$ [_____]

107 AVX LTD

AVX plc assembles circuit boards for use by high-technology audio video companies. One particular board is the CB45. Due to the rapidly advancing technology in this field, AVX plc is constantly being challenged to learn new techniques.

AVX plc initially priced each batch of CB45 circuit boards on the basis of its standard cost of $960 plus a mark-up of 25%.

Recently the company has noticed that, due to increasing competition, it is having difficulty maintaining its sales volume at this price.

The Finance Director has agreed that the long-run unit variable cost of the CB45 circuit board is $672.72 per batch. She has suggested that the price charged should be based on an analysis of market demand.

She has discovered that at a price of $1,200 the demand is 16 batches per month, for every $20 reduction in selling price there is an increase in demand of 1 batch of CB45 circuit boards, and for every $20 increase in selling price there is a reduction in demand of 1 batch.

The profit-maximising selling price per batch using the data supplied by the Finance Director is

$ [_____]

108   MtF

Company MtF is reviewing its pricing for one of its products.

The product's marginal costs are $25 per unit and MtF wish to set a price to maximise profits.

If the product's demand function is P=85 – 0.05X what is the profit maximising price and quantity?

A   Price = 55 and Quantity = 600

B   Price = 25 and Quantity = 600

C   Price = 45 and Quantity = 1,100

D   Price = 30 and Quantity = 1,100

109   Which of the following is NOT a weakness of the economist's pricing model (MC=MR).

A   It is difficult to identify the demand curve for a product

B   Other factors may affect demand

C   It takes account of the relationship between price and demand

D   A company's strategy may not be to maximise profit in the short term

110   From the pricing formula P = a – b X match the element to its correct description.

List 1 options	List 2 options
P	Profit maximising quantity
a	Slope of the demand curve
b	Profit maximising price
X	Intercept on the y axis (price where sales = zero)

111   Company TVC is calculating the price of a new product and wishes to use the economists pricing model P= a – bX to reach its profit maximising price.

Market research has determined that for $30 increase in price the demand will fall by 150 units and that maximum demand is 15,000 units.

The profit maximising quantity is 10,500. The profit maximising price is

$ [   ]

112   XYZ MOTOR GROUP

XYZ motor group comprises three autonomous divisions and its divisional managers are paid salary bonuses linked to the profit that their respective divisions achieve.

The New Vehicle (NV) division has a city showroom. It sells new vehicles and accepts trade-ins which are sold to the Used Vehicle (UV) division at a 'going trade price' less any necessary repair costs. The Vehicle Repair (VR) division performs necessary repair work to trade-ins and invoices UV for such work on a full cost plus basis. Both the UV and VR divisions do a great deal of business unrelated to trade-ins.

NV has the option of selling a new vehicle to a customer for $40,000 (including a 25% profit mark up on cost) providing the customer is given a trade-in value of $28,000 on their old vehicle. Reference to used car value guides indicate that the going trade price for the trade-in vehicle will be $17,500. However, it is estimated that UV division will be able to sell the trade in for $28,900 after incurring a charge from VR for repairing the vehicle as follows:

	$
Variable costs	500
Fixed overheads	250 (being 50% of VCs)
Mark up	75 (being 10% on cost)
Total	**825**

The impact on the contribution of the NV division and XYZ in total of proceeding with the new car sale on the terms specified is

```



```

The impact on the contribution of the UV division and XYZ in total of proceeding with the new car sale on the terms specified is

```



```

The impact on the contribution of the VR division and XYZ in total of proceeding with the new car sale on the terms specified is

```



```

The impact on the contribution of XYZ in total of proceeding with the new car sale on the terms specified is

```



```

C: MANAGING AND CONTROLLING THE PERFORMANCE OF ORGANISATIONAL UNITS

113   Division P is an investment centre within PC Ltd. Over which of the following is the manager of Division P likely to have control?

(i)   Transfer prices

(ii)   Level of inventory in the division

(iii)   Discretionary fixed costs incurred in the division

(iv)   Apportioned head office costs

A   (i), (ii), (iii) and (iv)

B   (i), (ii) and (iii) only

C   (i) and (ii) only

D   (i) only

114   Within decentralised organisations, there may be cost centres, investment centres and profit centres. Which of the following statements is true?

A   Cost centres have a higher degree of autonomy than profit centres

B   Investment centres have the highest degree of autonomy and cost centres the lowest

C   Investment centres have the lowest degree of autonomy

D   Profit centres have the highest degree of autonomy and cost centres the lowest

115   A company makes three products xx, yy and zz. The following information is available

	XX	YY	ZZ
	$	$	$
Sales	18,000	40,000	68,000
Variable costs	10,000	35,000	48,000
Fixed costs	5,000	9,000	14,000
Profit/(Loss)	3,000	(4,000)	6,000

It is believed that a percentage of the fixed costs relating to product YY are avoidable.

What is the minimum percentage of fixed costs that must be avoidable if the company is to cease producing product YY? (Calculate to the nearest whole percentage.)

116 HULME

Hulme has three divisions. Budgeted information for the forthcoming period is as follows:

	Division T $000	Division H $000	Division E $000	Total $000
Sales	700	560	150	1,410
Variable costs	(550)	(440)	(100)	(1,090)
Contribution	150	120	50	320
Fixed costs				450
Profit				(130)

Eighty per cent of the fixed costs are specific to each division being split between T, H and E in the ratio 3:4:1, respectively.

Which divisions should be kept open by Hulme given that their objective is to maximise profit?

117 A service company evaluates its performance using a number of key ratios. This includes the current ratio which is targeted not to fall below a value of 2.

Forecasts to date predict that receivables will fluctuate between $135,000 and $142,000, and payables between $17,000 and $22,000. The company has no inventory.

What is the maximum budgeted overdraft permitted if the company is to achieve its target?

$ [   ]

118 **A division has a return on investment of 18% and an asset turnover of two times. What is the division's net profit margin?**

119 **An organisation is divided into a number of divisions, each of which operates as a profit centre. Which of the following would be useful measures to monitor divisional performance?**

(i)   Contribution

(ii)   Controllable profit

(iii) Return on investment

(iv)   Residual income

(v)   Economic value added

A   (i) only

B   (i) and (ii) only

C   (iii), (iv) and (v) only

D   All of them

120 A company evaluates its performance using a number of key ratios. This includes the current ratio which is targeted not to fall below a value of 1.7.

Forecasts for the elements of working capital are inventory $14,800, receivables $19,600 and payables $144,000.

What is the minimum budgeted bank balance permitted if the company is to achieve its target?

$ [   ]

121 A division has a net profit margin of 16% and an asset turnover of 0.9 times.

What is the division's return on investment?

122 A company has an asset turnover of 5 and a net profit margin of 4%. It has profits of $80,000.

What is the value of its capital employed?

$ [   ]

123 Extracts from B's master budget for the latest period are as follows:

Income statement	$000
Revenue	5,440
Gross profit	2,730
Profit from operations	900
Balance sheet	
Non-current assets	1,850
Inventory	825
Receivables	710
Bank	50
Current liabilities	780

Calculate the following figures:

The operating profit margin for the budget period [   ] %

The total net asset turnover for the period [   ] times (2 d.p.)

The budgeted current ratio [   ] times (2 d.p.)

The budgeted quick (acid test) ratio [   ] times (2 d.p.)

124 DB HOLDINGS LTD

You have been asked to comment on the financial position of DB Holdings Ltd. You have obtained copies of the two most recent sets of the company's audited accounts which are summarised as follows:

All figures in $000	2013	2014
Equipment net of depreciation	2,400	2,200
Premises	1,600	900
Inventory	560	1,080
Receivables	320	980
Cash/(Overdraft)	160	−180
Payables	−280	−780
Net assets	4,760	4,200
Share capital	1,600	1,600
Loan from Directors	2,200	1,400
Cumulative retained profits	960	1,200
Capital	4,760	4,200
Revenue (sales)	4,800	5,800
Operating profit	320	420
Dividends paid	80	180

You know that due to the nature of the company's business, most of its business costs are purchases. The chairman of DB Holdings has recently quoted in the press:

DB Holdings has always been a profitable company. However, we are following a high growth strategy and this has put pressure on cash flow. We have a number of new clients signed up and believe the future is bright.

Calculate the following business metrics for DB Holdings Ltd. in 2013 (first column) and 2014 (second column)

ROCE

Profit margin on sales

Receivables days

Inventory days

Payables days

Cash conversion period

125 A company has set a target ROI of 12% for its divisions, this is deemed to represent the return necessary to benefit the company.

Division D achieved an ROI of 17% last year and is not expecting any major change from ongoing operations.

The purchase of a new piece of equipment has been proposed by a member of the production team. It is estimated that it will boost profits by $128,000 per annum for an investment of $855,000.

Is the divisional manager likely to accept or reject the investment? Will this be to the benefit or the detriment of the company?

126 A company has set a target ROI of 14% for its divisions, this is based on the company's cost of capital.

Division D achieved an ROI of 8% last year and is not expecting any major change from ongoing operations. However, a manager has suggested that cost savings of $15,000 per annum can be obtained by investing $135,000 in upgrading a particular piece of equipment.

Is the divisional manager likely to accept or reject the investment? Will this be to the benefit or the detriment of the company?

127 A company uses ROI to assess divisional performance, but it is considering switching to RI. The company's cost of capital is 15%.

Division C has an ROI of 21% which is not expected to change. An investment of $155,000 is available, which is expected to yield profits of $28,000 per annum.

Is the manager of division C likely to accept or reject the investment if ROI is used to assess performance? Would this change if RI was used?

128 Division G of a large company is approaching its year end. The division is evaluated using ROI with a target rate of return of 15%. The division has control of all aspects of its operation except that all cash balances are centralised by the company and therefore left off divisional balance sheets.

The divisional manager is considering the following options.

(i)   To delay payment of a supplier until next year, the potential prompt payment discount of 5% will be lost. The debt is for $27,500.

(ii)   To scrap a redundant asset with a book value of $147,000. The manager has been offered $15,000 as immediate scrap proceeds, whilst they are fairly confident that they could get $25,000 in an industry auction to be held at the start of the new year.

Assume that the manager is very short-termist (i.e. only considers the implications for this year) and that the expected ROI for the year, before these options, is 18%. Which of the following represents the most likely combination that the manager will choose?

	(i)	(ii)
A	Delay	Scrap now
B	Delay	Scrap next year
C	Do not delay	Scrap now
D	Do not delay	Scrap next year

129 A divisionalised company uses transfer pricing as part of its management information system. Each manager is assessed on their divisional profit.

Division A makes a unit for $10 variable cost and $3 of fixed cost is absorbed.

Division B takes these units, incurs another $8 variable cost and absorbs $4.

It then sells them for $21.

The transfer price is set at $12.

There are no capacity constraints and all fixed costs are unavoidable in the short run.

Select ALL that apply:

○ The manager of division A is likely to produce the units.

○ The manager of divisions B is likely to produce the units.

○ From the company's perspective, production should occur.

○ The transfer price is goal congruent.

130 **Which of the following is NOT a method of transfer pricing?**

A Cost plus transfer price

B Internal price

C Market-based transfer price

D Two part transfer price

131 TM plc makes components which it sells internally to its subsidiary RM Ltd, as well as to its own external market.

The external market price is $24.00 per unit, which yields a contribution of 40% of sales. For external sales, variable costs include $1.50 per unit for distribution costs, which are not incurred on internal sales. TM plc has sufficient capacity to meet all of the internal and external sales.

In order to maximise group profit, at what unit price should the component be transferred to RM Ltd?

$ [   ]

132 Division A makes alphas which are converted into betas by division B. A's variable costs are $150 per unit and B's are $80 per unit. B sells completed betas for $290 each. There is an intermediate market for alphas with a price of $180 which significantly exceeds the capacity of divisions A and B.

(i) **Assuming that B cannot buy from the market in alphas (but A can sell into the market), what is the widest range of TP that encourages the divisions to trade with each other?**

$ [   ]   to $ [   ]

(ii) **Assuming that A cannot sell into the market in alphas (but B can buy from the market), what is the widest range of TP that now encourages the divisions to trade with each other?**

$ [   ]   to $ [   ]

133 **One of the main reasons for adopting a decentralised organisation in preference to a centralised organisation structure is the:**

A improved goal congruence between the divisional manager's goals and the goals of the organisation

B availability of less subjective measures of performance

C improved communication of information among the organisation's managers

D rapid response of management to environmental changes

134 **A company has the following balance sheet totals at the end of its most recent financial year:**

	$million
Non-current assets	3.64
Current assets	0.42
Share capital and reserves*	2.69
Long-term debt	1.00
Current liabilities	0.37

* Includes retained profit for the year of $320,000 after deducting:

Ordinary share dividends	$200,000
Interest on long-term debt	$100,000
Taxation	$70,000

Calculate, to 1 d.p., the Return On Investment (ROI) of the company for the year (using end-year balance sheet values for investment).

| | %
|---|

135 A division of a company has capital employed of $2m and its return on capital is 12%. It is considering a new project requiring capital of $500,000 and is expected to yield profits of $90,000 per annum. The company's interest rate is 10%.

If the new project is accepted, the residual income of the division will be:

A $40,000

B $80,000

C $30,000

D $330,000

136 Division M has produced the following results in the last financial year:

		$000
Net profit		360
Capital employed:	Non-current assets	1,500
	Net current assets	100

For evaluation purposes all divisional assets are valued at original cost.

The division is considering a project which will increase annual net profit by $25,000, but will require average inventory levels to increase by $30,000 and non-current assets to increase by $100,000.

There is an 18% capital charge on investments.

Given these circumstances, will the evaluation criteria of Return on Investment (ROI) and Residual Income (RI) motivate Division M management to accept this project?

	ROI	RI
A	Yes	Yes
B	Yes	No
C	No	Yes
D	No	No

137 Summary financial statements are given below for one division of a large divisionalised company.

Summary divisional financial statements for the year to 31 December

Balance sheet		Income statement	
	$000		$000
Non-current assets	1,500	Revenue	4,000
Current assets	600	Operating costs	3,600
Total assets	2,100	Operating profit	400
		Interest paid	70
Divisional equity	1,000	Profit before tax	330
Long-term borrowings	700		
Current liabilities	400		
Total equity and liabilities	2,100		

The cost of capital for the division is estimated at 12% each year. Annual rate of interest on the long-term loans is 10%. All decisions concerning the division's capital structure are taken by central management.

The divisional Return on Investment (ROI) for the year ended 31 December is:

A 19.0%

B 19.4%

C 23.5%

D 33.0%

138 Summary financial statements are given below for one division of a large divisionalised company.

Summary divisional financial statements for the year to 31 December

Balance sheet		Income statement	
	$000		$000
Non-current assets	1,500	Revenue	4,000
Current assets	600	Operating costs	3,600
Total assets	2,100	Operating profit	400
		Interest paid	70
Divisional equity	1,000	Profit before tax	330
Long-term borrowings	700		
Current liabilities	400		
Total equity and liabilities	2,100		

The cost of capital for the division is estimated at 12% each year.

Annual rate of interest on the long-term loans is 10%.

All decisions concerning the division's capital structure are taken by central management.

The divisional Residual Income (RI) for the year ended 31 December is:

A $160,000

B $196,000

C $230,000

D $330,000

139 A division has net assets of $420,000. The profit statement for the division for the latest period is as follows:

	$
Revenue	630,000
Variable costs	390,000
Contribution	240,000
Attributable fixed costs	180,000
Allocated central costs	25,000
Divisional profit	35,000

The divisional manager is considering investing in a machine costing $50,000. The machine would earn annual profits, after depreciation, of $5,500. The company's cost of capital is 10%.

Calculate the division's controllable return on investment, without the new machine:

[   ] %

Calculate the division's controllable return on investment, with the new machine:

[   ] %

Calculate the controllable residual income for the division with the new machine:

$ [   ]

Calculate the controllable residual income for the division without the new machine:

$ [   ]

140 An investment centre has earned an accounting profit of $135,000, after charging historical cost depreciation of $22,000 and increasing the provision for doubtful debts by $8,000 to $12,000. If the non-current assets had been valued at replacement cost the depreciation charge would have been $41,000.

The net book value of the investment centre's net assets is $420,000 and the replacement cost is estimated to be $660,000. The organisation's risk adjusted cost of capital is 14% but it has a large bank loan which incurs annual interest charges of 10%.

Ignoring taxation, the economic value added (EVA) for the investment centre is:

A $29,920

B $31,040

C $31,600

D $56,800

141 Division G has reported annual operating profits of $20.2 million. This was after charging $3 million for the full cost of launching a new product that is expected to last three years.

Division G has a risk adjusted cost of capital of 11% and is paying interest on a substantial bank loan at 8%. The historical cost of the assets in Division G, as shown on its balance sheet, is $60 million, and the replacement cost has been estimated at $84 million.

Ignore the effects of taxation.

What would be the EVA for Division G?

A $15.4 million

B $11.48 million

C $10.6 million

D $12.74 million

142 The following data have been extracted from a company's year-end accounts:

	$
Turnover	7,055,016
Gross profit	4,938,511
Operating profit	3,629,156
Non-current assets	4,582,000
Cash at bank	4,619,582
Short term borrowings	949,339
Trade receivables	442,443
Trade payables	464,692

Calculate the following four performance measures:

(i)   Operating profit margin

(ii)   Return on capital employed

(iii)   Trade receivable days (debtors days)

(iv)   Current (Liquidity) ratio

143 **Which of the following best describes an investment centre?**

A   A centre for which managers are accountable only for costs.

B   A centre for which managers are accountable only for financial outputs in the form of generating sales revenue.

C   A centre for which managers are accountable for profit.

D   A centre for which managers are accountable for profit and current and non-current assets.

144 ABC has two profit centres, Centre 1 and Centre 2. Centre 1 transfers one third of its output to Centre 2 and sells the remainder on the external market for $28 per unit. The transfers to Centre 2 are at a transfer price of cost plus 20%.

Centre 2 incurs costs of $8 per unit in converting the transferred unit, which is then sold to external customers for $40 per unit. Centre 1 costs are $20 per unit and the budgeted output for period 6 is 450 units. There is no budgeted change in inventories for either profit centre.

The budgeted results for Centre 1 and Centre 2 for period 6 will be:

	Centre 1	**Centre 2**
A	$1,800 profit	$2,400 profit
B	$3,000 profit	$1,200 profit
C	$3,000 profit	$4,800 profit
D	$3,900 profit	$2,400 profit

145 Which of the following statements about market-based transfer prices are correct?

(i)   A profit centre buying the item is likely to be indifferent between buying externally and buying the item from within the business.

(ii)   A transfer price at market value might not encourage profit centres buying the item to utilise spare capacity.

A   (i) only

B   (ii) only

C   Both (i) and (ii)

D   Neither (i) nor (ii)

146 X plc, a manufacturing company, has two divisions: Division A and Division B. Division A produces one type of product, ProdX, which it transfers to Division B and also sells externally. Division B has been approached by another company which has offered to supply 2,500 units of ProdX for $35 each. The following details for Division A are available:

	$
Sales revenue	
Sales to Division B @ $40 per unit	400,000
External sales @ $45 per unit	270,000
Less:	
Variable cost @ $22 per unit	352,000
Fixed costs	100,000
	———
Profit	218,000
	———

External sales of Prod X cannot be increased, and division B decides to buy from the other company.

The annual (increase/reduction)* in divisional profit for Division A amounts to:

$ [   ]

The annual (increase/reduction)* in profit for Company X amounts to:

$ [   ]

(*) Delete as appropriate

147 X and Y are two divisions of Newtyle. Division X manufactures one product, Alpha. Unit production cost and market price are as follows:

	$
Direct materials	6
Direct labour	4
Fixed overhead	1
	11
Prevailing market price	$16

Product Alpha is sold outside the company in a perfectly competitive market and also to Division Y. If sold outside the company, Alpha incurs variable selling costs of $2 per unit which are not incurred on internal transfers.

If the total demand for Alpha were more than sufficient for Division X to manufacture to capacity, at what price would the company prefer Division X to transfer Alpha to Division Y?

A $10

B $11

C $14

D $16

148 Division A transfers 100,000 units of a component to Division B each year. The market price of the component is $25 per unit.

Division A's variable cost is $15 per unit. Its fixed costs are $500,000 each year.

What price per unit would be credited to Division A for each component that it transfers to Division B under marginal cost pricing and under two-part tariff pricing (where the Divisions have agreed that the fixed fee will be $200,000)?

	Marginal cost pricing	Two-part tariff pricing
A	$15	$15
B	$25	$15
C	$15	$25
D	$25	$25

149 Division S transfers 75,000 units of a component to Division T each year. The market price of the component is $40. Division S's variable cost is $28 per unit. Division S's fixed costs are $380,000 each year.

What price would be credited to Division S for each component that it transfers to Division T under:

(a) Two-part tariff pricing (where the Divisions have agreed that the fixed fee will be $160,000)?

(b) Dual pricing (based on marginal cost and market price)?

	Two-part tariff pricing	Dual pricing
A	$12	$28
B	$12	$40
C	$28	$40
D	$33	$28

150 CD Globes transferred 11,000 units of product N from its manufacturing division in Canada to its selling division in the UK during the year just ended.

The manufacturing cost of each unit of product N was $120 (75% of which was variable cost). The market price for each unit of product N in Canada was $300. The Canada division's profit after tax for its sales to the UK division for the year ended was $1,100,000.

The UK division incurred marketing and distribution costs of £40 for each unit of product N and sold the product for £250 a unit. The UK tax rate was 25%. (Exchange rate: £1 = $1.50)

If product N had been transferred at the Canadian market price, the tax rate in Canada must have been (to the nearest percentage point):

A 32%

B 36%

C 40%

D 44%

151 CD Globes transferred 11,000 units of product N from its manufacturing division in Canada to its selling division in the UK during the year just ended.

The manufacturing cost of each unit of product N was $120 (75% of which was variable cost). The market price for each unit of product N in Canada was $300. The Canada division's profit after tax for its sales to the UK division for the year ended was $1,100,000.

The UK division incurred marketing and distribution costs of £40 for each unit of product N and sold the product for £250 a unit. The UK tax rate was 25%. (Exchange rate: £1 = $1.50)

If the transfers had been made at variable cost, the UK division's profit after tax would have been:

A £950,000

B £987,500

C £1,050,000

D £1,237,500

152 CMW Ltd is a UK holding company with an overseas subsidiary. The directors of CMW Ltd wish to transfer profits from the UK to the overseas company.

They are considering changing the level of transfer prices charged on goods shipped from the overseas subsidiary to CMW Ltd and the size of the royalty payments paid by CMW Ltd to its subsidiary.

In order to transfer profit from CMW Ltd to the overseas subsidiary, the directors of CMW Ltd should:

A   Increase both the transfer prices and royalty payments

B   Increase the transfer prices but decrease royalty payments

C   Decrease the transfer prices but increase royalty payments

D   Decrease both the transfer prices and royalty payments

153 WX has two divisions, Y and Z. The following budgeted information is available.

Division Y manufactures motors and budgets to transfer 60,000 motors to Division Z and to sell 40,000 motors to external customers.

Division Z assembles food mixers and uses one motor for each food mixer produced.

The standard cost information per motor for Division Y is as follows:

	$
Direct materials	70
Direct labour	20
Variable production overhead	10
Fixed production overhead	40
Fixed selling and administration overhead	10
Total standard cost	150

In order to set the external selling price the company uses a 33.33% mark up on total standard cost.

Calculate:

The budgeted profit/(loss) for Division Y if the transfer price is set at marginal cost:

$ [   ]

The budgeted profit/(loss) for Division Y if the transfer price is set at the total production cost:

$ [   ]

SUBJECT P2 : ADVANCED MANAGEMENT ACCOUNTING

154 The KL Company provides legal and secretarial services to small businesses. KL has two divisions.

Secretarial Division

This division provides secretarial services to external clients and to the Legal Division. It charges all its clients, including the Legal Division, at a rate of $40 per hour. The marginal cost of one hour of secretarial services is $20.

Legal Division

The Legal Division provides legal services. One service, called L&S, involves a combination of legal and secretarial services. Each hour of L&S charged to clients involves one hour of legal services and one hour of secretarial services. The secretarial element of this service is purchased from the Secretarial Division. The likely demand for L&S at different prices is as follows:

Demand (hours)	Price per hour ($)
0	100
1,000	90
2,000	80
3,000	70
4,000	60
5,000	50

The marginal cost of one hour of legal services is $25.

Calculate the level of sales (hours) and total contribution of L&S that would maximise the profit from this service FOR THE LEGAL DIVISION. Assume the Legal Division pays the Secretarial Division at a rate of $40 per hour for secretarial services.

	hours (level of sales)

	contribution

Calculate the level of sales (hours) and total contribution that would maximise the profit from L&S FOR THE KL COMPANY AS A WHOLE.

	hours (level of sales)

	contribution

155 The annual operating statement for a company is shown below:

	$000
Sales revenue	800
Less variable costs	390
Contribution	410
Less fixed costs	90
Less depreciation	20
Net income	300

Assets	$6.75m

The cost of capital is 13% per annum. The return on investment (ROI) for the company is closest to:

A   4.44%

B   4.74%

C   5.77%

D   6.07%

156 The annual operating statement for a company is shown below:

	$000
Sales revenue	800
Less variable costs	390
Contribution	410
Less fixed costs	90
Less depreciation	20
Net income	300

Assets	$6.75m

The cost of capital is 13% per annum.

The residual income (RI) for the company is closest to (in $000):

A   (467)

B   (487)

C   (557)

D   (577)

157 A company has reported annual operating profits for the year of $89.2m after charging $9.6m for the full development costs of a new product that is expected to last for the current year and two further years. The cost of capital is 13% per annum.

The balance sheet at the start of the year showed fixed assets with a historical cost of $120m. A note to the balance sheet estimates that the replacement cost of these fixed assets at the beginning of the current year was $168m. The assets have been depreciated at 20% per year (based on historical cost). Depreciation at 20% of replacement cost is considered to be a reasonable estimate for economic depreciation.

The company has working capital of $27.2m based on a replacement cost valuation at the end of the year.

Ignore the effects of taxation. The Economic Value Added® (EVA) of the company at the end of the current year is closest to:

A $64.16m

B $70.56m

C $83.36m

D $100.96m

158 ZP plc operates two subsidiaries, X and Y. X is a component-manufacturing subsidiary and Y is an assembly and final product subsidiary. Both subsidiaries produce one type of output only. Subsidiary Y needs one component from subsidiary X for every unit of Product W produced. Subsidiary X transfers to Subsidiary Y all of the components needed to produce Product W. Subsidiary X also sells components on the external market.

The following budgeted information is available for each subsidiary:

	X	Y
Market price per component	$800	
Market price per unit of W		$1,200
Production costs per component	$600	
Assembly costs per unit of W		$400
Non production fixed costs	$1.5m	$1.3m
External demand	10,000 units	12,000 units
Capacity	22,000 units	
Taxation rates	25%	30%

The production cost per component is 60% variable. The fixed production costs are absorbed based on budgeted output.

X sets a transfer price at marginal cost plus 70%.

Calculate the post-tax profit generated by each subsidiary.

OBJECTIVE TEST QUESTIONS : SECTION 1

159 Pick **TWO** strengths of using Return on Investment as a performance measure for Investment appraisal:

○ It is an absolute measure of increase in shareholder wealth

○ It is commonly used and understood

○ It uses objective profits instead of subjective cash flows

○ It leads to goal congruent decisions

○ It cannot be manipulated

○ It can be used to compare projects of different sizes

160 Division X's performance is based on return on investment (ROI) calculated using figures controllable by the division. Calculate, to 2 decimal places, the ROI % for division X based on the following figures:

Net profit $675,000; Capital employed $10m

Included in net profit are:

Depreciation on division X's assets of $200,000

Depreciation on head office assets of $250,000

Financing costs of $100,000 to represent division X's share of a loan taken out by the company to restructure its financing structure.

161 The following statements have been made with regards to the Return On Investment measure.

Select ALL that apply:

(i) Projects with a return on investment that beats the company's cost of capital should always be accepted

(ii) Return on investment is a useful tool for evaluating profit centres

(iii) Return on investment is best calculated using profit after tax

(iv) Return on investment can be broken down into secondary measures of performance

162 A divisional manager currently earning a return on investment (ROI) of 18% is offered a project with the following cash flows:

Purchase of machinery (at the start of the project): $600,000

Revenue: $20,000 per month

Variable costs: $5,000 per month

Life of project: 5 years

Sale of machinery at end of project: $100,000

The manager is evaluated on their ability to improve ROI. Based on the ROI the manager will achieve at the end of the 1st year of the project (assuming all other divisional activities carry on generating a ROI of 18%), should the project be accepted?

Select the correct answer below:

A   Yes, because the project return is greater than the company's cost of capital

B   Yes, because the project ROI is 36%, which is greater than the current return

C   Yes, because the project makes a profit over its life

D   No, because the project ROI is 16% which is lower than the current return

163   A new division has the following figures in relation to its first year:

Annual cash flows: $20,000

Assets invested at start of year: $50,000

Residual value: $5,000

Depreciation policy for assets: Straight line over 5 years

Calculate the return on investment earned by the division as at the end of its first year to the nearest whole %

	%

164   **Pick TWO strengths of using Residual Income as a performance measure for a large organisation/group:**

A   It brings home the cost of financing to the divisional manager

B   It is commonly used and understood

C   It uses objective profits instead of subjective cash flows

D   It often leads to goal congruent decisions

E   It cannot be manipulated

F   It can be used to compare divisions of different sizes

165   A division currently has an annual return on investment (ROI) of 20% on its investment base of $1,200,000. The following additional projects are being considered:

Project	Investment outlay, in $000	Annual profit in $000	ROI%
A	300	100	33
B	700	210	30
C	500	130	26
D	200	44	22

Which combination of investments will maximise the division's return on investment, assuming no capital rationing is in place?

A   All four projects

B   A, B and C only

C   A and B only

D   A only

166 **Which of the following statements correctly explains the situation where a company faces capital rationing?**

A   Investment funds are unlimited

B   Funds are available to undertake all beneficial projects but a minimum target return on projects has been imposed

C   Insufficient funds are available to undertake all beneficial projects

D   No further funds are available for capital expenditure

167 A divisional manager currently earning a return on investment of 15% is offered a project with the following cash flows:

Purchase of machinery: $100,000   Revenue: $7,500 per month

Variable costs: $4,900 per month   Life of project: 5 years

Sale of machinery at end of project: $10,000   Depreciation method: straight line

The divisional manager's bonus is based on the Residual Income achieved by the division and is senior enough to influence the manager's decisions. The company's cost of capital is 12%.

Would the manager accept this project?

A   No, because the project has a negative Residual Income

B   Yes, because the project has a positive Residual Income

C   Yes, because the project makes a profit over its life

D   No, because the Return on Investment is 13.2% and is less than the division's current Return on Investment

168 **The following statements have been made in relation to ROI and RI. Select ALL that apply:**

(i)   Residual income will always increase when investments earning a return higher than the cost of capital is undertaken.

(ii) Return on investment will always increase when investments earning a return higher than the cost of capital are undertaken.

(iii) Using residual income as a performance measure allows easy comparison between divisions.

(iv) Return on investment will artificially increase over time if net book values of assets are included in the calculation of capital employed.

169 **Calculate the controllable Residual Income (to the nearest $000) of division J (an investment centre) based on the following figures in ($000):**

Gross profit	1,000
Operating expenses	600 (see note 1)
Net profit	400
Interest	50 (see note 2)
Profit before tax	350
Tax	25 (see note 2)
Profit after tax	325

Note 1: Within operating expenses is included $250,000 as a share of head office expenses, made up of an administration recharge of $100,000 and depreciation of $150,000.

Note 2: Both interest and tax are calculated at company level and apportioned appropriately to the divisions

Capital employed by J:

Net assets   3,000

Net assets comprise the division J factory, worth $2m, and the division J office (which is an allocated floor of head office) worth $1m. The cost of capital of the company is 20%.

170   A divisional manager is offered 2 projects:

Project A: Invest $50,000 to upgrade production machinery to be more efficient. The current net book value of the machinery is $1 million.

Contribution earned should increase by 20% from its current level of $100,000 per annum.

The upgrade will last for 4 years after which the machinery will be scrapped for $0 and replaced with new machinery.

Project B: Invest $1.5 million to buy a patent that will allow an upgraded version of the current product to be sold. Revenue per annum will increase from $1m per annum to $1.5m.

Variable costs will be 60% of revenue. Company policy is to capitalise patents and depreciate them on a straight line basis over their useful lives. The patent will lapse after 50 years.

The company cost of capital is 13%. What decision will the divisional manager take if divisional evaluated based on residual income?

A   Accept both projects

B   Reject both projects

C   Accept A and reject B

D   Accept B and reject A

171   **Why would a company want to encourage the use of non-financial performance indicators?**

A   To encourage short-termism

B   To look at the fuller picture of the business

C   To enable results to be easily manipulated to the benefit of the manager

D   To prevent goal congruence

172 **Complete the following text by selecting the missing words and phrases (the same word may be used more than once):**

all	profitability	cost	returning customers
income from new products	non-financial	customer satisfaction	innovation and learning
efficiency	internal business	financial	survival

The balanced scorecard approach is a way of providing information to management which involves the inclusion of _____ information alongside financial information.

It emphasises the need to provide the user with a set of information which addresses _____ relevant areas of performance in an objective and unbiased fashion.

Although the specific measures used may vary, a scorecard would normally include the following measures

- _____ – the financial perspective

- _____ – the customer perspective

- innovation – the _____ perspective

- internal efficiency – the _____ perspective.

By providing all this information in a single report, management is able to assess the impact of particular actions on all perspectives of the company's activities. Under each perspective, a company should state its aims and specify measures of performance.

For example:

		Aims	**Measure**
1	Financial perspective	_____	Current ratio
2	Customer perspective	Satisfaction	_____
3	Internal business perspective	_____	Throughput rates
4	Innovation and learning	New products	_____

173 **Which ONE of the following is not a perspective that is monitored by the Balanced Scorecard approach to performance measurement?**

A   Financial

B   Customer

C   Supplier

D   Innovation and learning

174 **The following statements have been made about performance measures. Select ALL that apply:**

(i)   If a company uses a balanced scorecard approach to provide information, it will not use ROI or Residual Income as divisional performance measures.

(ii)   The residual income will always increase when investments earning above the cost of capital are undertaken.

(iii)   The internal business perspective of the Balanced Scorecard approach to the provision of information is concerned only with the determination of internal transfer prices that will encourage goal congruent decisions.

(iv)   An advantage of the residual income performance measure is that it facilitates comparisons between investment centres.

175   A and B are two divisions of a company. A makes two products, Product A and Product B. Product A is commercialised outside the company. Product B is only sold to Division B, at a unit transfer price of $176. Unit costs for Product B are as follows:

	$
Variable materials	60
Variable labour	40
Variable overheads	40
Fixed overheads	20
	160

Division B has received an offer from another company to supply a substitute for Product B, for $152 per unit.

Assuming Division A can sell as much of Product A as it can produce and the unit profitability of Products A and B are equal, what will be the effects on profits if Division B accepts the offer?

A   Profit in Division A would not change and the overall company profit would decrease.

B   Profit in Division A would decrease and the overall company profit would not change.

C   Profit in Division A would not change and the overall company profit would increase.

D   Profit in Division A would increase and the overall company profit would not change.

176 U PLC

U plc uses Return on Investment (ROI) to assess its divisional performance. U plc estimates that the net cash flows associated with a new piece of machinery will be equal in each of the five years of the asset's life, but the company's figures for capital employed and accounting profit have come under scrutiny.

Which methods of stating these two components of ROI will provide figures which are constant from year to year over the five year life of this new asset?

	Capital employed	**Accounting profit**
A	Gross book value	Profit after charging depreciation on a reducing balance basis
B	Gross book value	Profit after charging depreciation on a straight line basis
C	Net book value	Profit after charging depreciation on a straight line basis
D	Net book value	Profit after charging depreciation on a reducing balance basis

177 MCG PLC

In order to regain a competitive position, the Managing Director of MCG plc, a divisionalised business, has been advised to reduce the range of products and the product lines by about 20% to increase profits by at least 40%. To implement such a product divestment strategy could, they fear, alienate customers. They need to know which products need to be removed and which products are important to the survival of the company. They are unhappy about the overall performance of the company's activities. Benchmarking has been recommended as a method of assessing how the company's performance compares with that of their competitors.

Select ALL statements that are TRUE and apply to MCG plc:

○ **Internal benchmarking** can compare different divisions within MCG: some centres may be more profitable than others.

○ **Internal benchmarking could result in** a transfer of knowledge and skills and could be beneficial to the group as a whole.

○ **Competitive benchmarking** attempts to compare products, processes and results and show where the company is failing with reference to those of competitors.

○ **Customer benchmarking** attempts to compare corporate performance with the performance expected by customers.

178

Value for money is an important objective for not-for-profit organisations.

Which of the following actions is consistent with increasing value for money?

A Using a cheaper source of goods and thereby decreasing the quality of not-for-profit organisation services

B Searching for ways to diversify the finances of the not-for-profit organisation

C Decreasing waste in the provision of a service by the not-for-profit organisation

D Focusing on meeting the financial objectives of the not-for-profit organisation

D: RISK AND CONTROL

179 Indicate, by clicking in the relevant boxes, whether the following statements about attitudes to risk are true or false.

Statements	True	False
Only risk seekers will invest in risky projects.		
If an investment has a 60% chance of earning $100 and a 40% chance of losing $20, a risk neutral investor would be willing to pay $52 to make that investment.		
If an investment has a 60% chance of earning $100 and a 40% chance of losing $20, a risk averse investor would be willing to pay $52 to make that investment.		

180 A firm finds that the internal rate of return on a project is 10%, having assumed an inflation rate of 4% on all of its cash flows.

If it revises its estimate of inflation to 9%, what would be the revised internal rate of return on the project?

A   9.5%

B   15.3%

C   10.0%

D   13.0%

181 A local authority is considering automating the purchases system in several departments. Details of the proposed project are as follows:

Life of project:	5 years
Initial cost	$75,000

Annual savings:

Labour costs	$20,000
Other costs	$5,000
Cost of capital	15% per annum

The IRR for this project is nearest to:

A   10.13%

B   14.87%

C   15.64%

D   19.88%

E   20.13%

182 **The percentage change in the annual labour cost savings that could occur before the project ceases to be viable is**

A   10.50%

B   11.73%

C   13.13%

D   35.20%

E   44.00%

183 Company DW is considering a new project which has a projected NPV of $8,800 over an expected life of 5 years.

DW's cost of capital is 10% per annum. Labour cost for the project are $20,000 pa.

The percentage change in labour cost to two decimal places that could occur before the project becomes unviable is

A   11.61%

B   44.00%

C   8.80%

D   12.00%

184 Company FWM has appraised a project with an expected life of six years using NPV and has calculated the project has a negative NPV of $7,500. Few of the costs are controllable however the production director thinks that labour costs could be reduced. Labour currently costs $25,000 pa and FWM's cost of capital is 15%.

Calculate to two decimal places what percentage the labour costs must be reduced in order to make the project breakeven:

185 **In an NPV analysis, which THREE of the following advantages are associated with the use of sensitivity analysis in assessing the project cash flows?**

A   Calculates the extent by which a variable would need to change before the decision would change

B   Calculates the probability that a variable will change

C   Provides clear criteria for decision making

D   Identifies areas which are crucial to the success of the project

E   Facilitates subjective judgement

186 **Which of the following is NOT an advantage of sensitivity analysis?**

A   It is easy to calculate

B   Identifies critical cash flows

C   Gives management more information for decision making

D   Gives an indication of the likelihood of a variable changing

187 LFF plc are considering a new project with a five year life span. Due to the unpredictable supply of a key component, the production director has identified three possible levels of variable cost per unit:

Cost	Probability
Optimistic :$30	0.3
Likely: $35	0.5
Pessimistic:$45	0.2

Sales of 10,000 pa are expected. LFF PLC use a cost of capital of 12% to appraise projects.

What is the expected present value of the variable cost to be used in the NPV analysis to the nearest $?

A $1,300,000

B $1,279,775

C $201,285

D $355,000

188 CBG Co is considering a new project with an initial outlay of $80,000. There are several possible market conditions with their associated probabilities.

		Year 1 cash	Year 2 cash
Optimistic	30%	$70,000	$85,000
Most likely	45%	$40,000	$55,000
Pessimistic	25%	$25,000	$30,000

CBG Co evaluate their projects using a cost of capital of 10%. To the nearest $, what is the NPV of the project?

$ [   ]

189 A company is considering investing in a manufacturing project that would have a three year life span. The investment would involve an immediate cash outflow of $50,000, and have a zero residual value. In each of the three years, 4,000 units would be produced and sold. The contribution per unit, based on current prices, is $5. The company has an annual cost of capital of 8%. It is expected that the inflation rate will be 3% in each of the next three years.

The net present value of the project (to the nearest $500) is:

A $4,500

B $5,000

C $5,500

D $6,000

E $6,500

190 A company is considering investing in a manufacturing project that would have a three year life span. The investment would involve an immediate cash outflow of $50,000, and have a zero residual value. In each of the three years, 4,000 units would be produced and sold. The contribution per unit, based on current prices, is $5. The company has an annual cost of capital of 8%. It is expected that the inflation rate will be 3% in each of the next three years.

If the annual inflation rate is now projected to be 4%, the maximum monetary cost of capital for this project to remain viable is (to the nearest 0.5%)

A   13.0%

B   13.5%

C   14.0%

D   14.5%

191 A company is evaluating a new product proposal. The proposed product selling price is $220 per unit and the variable costs are $55 per unit. The incremental cash fixed costs for the product will be $190,000 per annum. The discounted cash flow calculations results in a positive NPV:

		Cash flow	Discount rate	Present value
		$		$
Year 0	Initial outlay	(2,000,000)	1.000	(2,000,000)
Year 1–6	Annual cash flow	450,000	4.623	2,080,350
Year 6	Sale of assets	75,000	0.630	47,250
Net present value				127,600

What is the percentage change in selling price that would result in the project having a net present value of zero?

A   3.2%

B   4.6%

C   5.9%

D   7.0%

192 A company is carrying out sensitivity analysis on an investment project. The initial DCF analysis, at a cost of capital of 10%, is as follows:

Year	Item	Cash flow	Discount factor at 10%	PV
		$		$
0	Cost of machine	(50,000)	1.000	(50,000)
1	Net cash flow from sales	22,000	0.909	19,998
2	Net cash flow from sales	22,000	0.826	18,172
3	Net cash flow from sales	10,000	0.751	7,510
3	Residual value of the machine	10,000	0.751	7,510
NPV				+ 3,190

The investment is in a machine that will make a product, Product Q. Product Q will sell for $40 per unit, and will have a variable cost of $10 per unit. Annual sales will be 1,000 units in years 1 and 2, and 600 units in year 3. Additional fixed cost expenditure on cash items will be $8,000 each year.

The residual value of the machine will be 20% of the initial cost of the machine.

To the nearest 0.1%, by how much could the selling price per unit of the product fall short of the expected $40 without the project ceasing to be viable, given no change in any of the other cash flow estimates?

A   3.6%

B   6.0%

C   6.1%

D   7.0%

193 A company is carrying out sensitivity analysis on an investment project. The initial DCF analysis, at a cost of capital of 10%, is as follows:

Year	Item	Cash flow	Discount factor at 10%	PV
		$		$
0	Cost of machine	(50,000)	1.000	(50,000)
1	Net cash flow from sales	22,000	0.909	19,998
2	Net cash flow from sales	22,000	0.826	18,172
3	Net cash flow from sales	10,000	0.751	7,510
3	Residual value of the machine	10,000	0.751	7,510
NPV				+ 3,190

The investment is in a machine that will make a product, Product Q. Product Q will sell for $40 per unit, and will have a variable cost of $10 per unit. Annual sales will be 1,000 units in years 1 and 2, and 600 units in year 3. Additional fixed cost expenditure on cash items will be $8,000 each year.

The residual value of the machine will be 20% of the initial cost of the machine.

To the nearest $1,000, what is the maximum amount that the machine can cost, without the project ceasing to be viable, given no change in any of the other cash flow estimates?

A $53,000

B $54,000

C $55,000

D $56,000

194 **Which of the following statements correctly describes the treatment of depreciation in investment appraisal calculations?**

    A   Depreciation should never be included in investment appraisal calculations

    B   Depreciation should never be included in discounted cash flow calculations

    C   Only depreciation charges relating to future investments should be included in discounted cash flow calculations

    D   Depreciation should be included in all investment appraisal calculations as it represents a notional cost

    E   Depreciation is included in investment appraisal where the company uses ARR as it is needed to calculate average annual profits. However it should never be included in discounted cash flow calculations as it is an accounting adjustment not a cash flow

195 **In NPV investment appraisal, which of the following project conditions would alter the assumptions underlying the standard treatment of the effects of taxation?**

    A   The company overall is not making taxable profits

    B   Corporation tax is paid quarterly

    C   When assets are sold they are priced at their written down value

    D   Investments are usually made over a period of two years

196 A financial services company is calculating the NPV of a project to develop a new medical insurance division. The division is to be located within the head office building and, as the company had been considering renting out the floor space, a rent charge will be applied based on local market rents.

What is the correct treatment of the rental charge?

    A   Not a relevant cost because rental payments are fixed costs.

    B   Not a relevant cost because the cost is a notional cost only

    C   A relevant cost because rent is a future cash flow.

    D   A relevant cost because all costs associated with the proposed division must be included.

197 A project has a net present value of $320,000.

The sales revenues for the project have a total pre-discounted value of $900,000 and a total present value of $630,000 after tax.

The sensitivity of the investment to changes in the value of sales is closest to:

    A $310,000

    B $580,000

    C   51%

    D   36%

198 An education authority is considering the implementation of a CCTV (closed circuit television) security system in one of its schools.

Details of the proposed project are as follows:

Life of project   5 years

Initial cost $75,000

Annual savings:

	Labour costs	$20,000
	Other costs	$5,000

Cost of capital   15% per annum

Calculate:

The internal rate of return for this project:

☐ %

The percentage change in the annual labour cost savings that could occur before the project ceased to be viable:

☐ %

199 The management accountant of Bar Company has estimated that the cash flows for Project X would be as follows:

Year	Investment $	Running costs $	Savings $
0	(120,000)		
1		(80,000)	150,000
2		(100,000)	160,000
3		(120,000)	170,000
4		(150,000)	180,000

The project has a positive NPV of $22,900 when discounted at the company's cost of capital, which is 20% per annum.

On reviewing the cost estimates, the management accountant decides that the running costs will in fact be 20% higher each year than originally estimated, although savings will be higher too.

Calculate the minimum percentage that annual savings must be higher than originally estimated for the project to remain viable.

☐ %

200 Shuffles is attempting to decide which size of fork-lift truck to buy in its warehouses. There are three grades of truck, the A series, B series and the C series. The uncertainty faced is the expected growth in the on-line market it serves, which could grow at 15%, 30% or even 40% in the next period.

Shuffles Limited has correctly produced the following decision table and has calculated the average daily contribution gained from each combination of truck and growth assumption.

Decision table		Type of truck		
		A series	**B series**	**C series**
Growth rate	15%	$2,400	$1,800	$3,600
	30%	$1,400	$1,900	$4,500
	40%	$4,900	$2,800	$3,900

Which truck would the pessimistic buyer get?

Which truck would the optimistic buyer get?

If the buyer were prone to regretting decisions that have been made which truck would they get?

If the probabilities of the given growth rates are

15%: 0.4, 30%: 0.25 and 40%: 0.35, which truck would the risk neutral buyer get?

201 A company is planning its investment schedule and intends to use Monte Carlo simulation to assist in the decision-making process.

Which of the following statements best describes the output from a Monte Carlo simulation?

A   A range of possible outcomes with associated probabilities

B   The expected economic yield of an investment

C   A project ranking which will maximise the company's NPV per $1 invested

D   The amount that should be spent to acquire perfect information about an outcome

202 The following statements have been made about the use of simulation.

Select ALL that apply:

○ Simulation models the behaviour of a system.

○ Simulation models can be used to study alternative solutions to a problem.

○ The equations describing the operating characteristics of the system are known.

○ A simulation model cannot prescribe what should be done about a problem.

203 A company can make either of two new products, X and Y, but not both. The profitability of each product depends on the state of the market, as follows:

Market state	Profit from product		Probability of market state
	X $	Y $	
Good	20,000	17,000	0.2
Fair	15,000	16,000	0.5
Poor	6,000	7,000	0.3

What is the expected value of perfect information as to the state of the market?

A $0

B $600

C $800

D $1,000

204 A company is considering the development and marketing of a new product. Development costs will be $2m. There is a 75% probability that the development effort will be successful, and a 25% probability that it will be unsuccessful. If development is successful and the product is marketed, it is estimated that:

	Expected profit	Probability
Product very successful	$6.0m	0.4
Product moderately successful	$1.8m	0.4
Product unsuccessful	($5.0m)	0.2

What is the expected value of the project?

A   ($0.41m)

B $2.12m

C $1.59m

D $0.12m

OBJECTIVE TEST QUESTIONS : SECTION 1

205 Dough Distributors has decided to increase its daily muffin purchases by 100 boxes. A box of muffins costs $2 and sells for $3 through regular stores. Any boxes not sold through regular stores are sold through Dough's thrift store for $1. Dough assigns the following probabilities to selling additional boxes:

Additional sales	Probability
60 boxes	60%
100 boxes	40%

What is the expected value of Dough's decision to buy 100 additional boxes of muffins?

A $52

B $68

C $28

D $40

206 To assist in an investment decision, Gift Co. selected the most likely sales volume from several possible outcomes.

Which of the following attributes would that selected sales volume reflect?

A   The greatest probability

B   The expected value

C   The mid-point of the range

D   The median

207 Your client wants your advice on which of two alternatives they should choose. One alternative is to sell an investment now for $10,000. An alternative is to hold the investment three days after which they can sell it for a certain selling price based on the following probabilities:

Selling price	Probability
$5,000	40%
$8,000	20%
$12,000	30%
$30,000	10%

Using probability theory, which of the following is the most reasonable statement?

A   Hold the investment three days because the expected value of holding exceeds the current selling price.

B   Hold the investment three days because of the chance of getting $30,000 for it.

C   Sell the investment now because the current selling price exceeds the expected value of holding.

D   Sell the investment now because there is a 60% chance that the selling price will fall in three days.

208 Leslie Company is an intermediary supplier of parts to several manufacturing companies. As the accounting consultant for Leslie Company you have compiled data on the day-to-day demand rate from Leslie's customers for Product A and the lead time to receive Product A from its supplier. The data are summarized in the following probability tables:

Demand for Product A

Unit demand per day	Probability of occurrence
0	45%
1	15%
2	30%
3	10%

Lead time for Product A

Lead time in days	Probability of occurrence
1	40%
2	35%
3	25%

Leslie is able to deliver Product A to its customers the same day that Product A is received from its supplier. All units of Product A demanded but not available, due to a stock-out, are backordered and are filled immediately when a new shipment arrives.

The probability of the demand for Product A being nine units during a 3-day lead time for delivery from the supplier is:

A 0.00025

B 0.10

C 0.025

D 0.25

209 A company knows that sales for a new product will either be at a high level, or at a low level. There is a 65% chance that sales will be at a high level. A market research company will predict the future sales level. Their forecasts are known to be correct 85% of the time.

If the company receives a forecast of low sales from the market researchers, what is the probability that they will subsequently achieve high sales?

A 75.32%

B 9.75%

C 39.5%

D 29.75%

E 24.68%

210 30% of the new cakes of a particular recipe are supplied from bakery A, the other 70% from bakery B. 10% of the cakes from Bakery A are not baked properly (they decompose when they are taken out of their box). 12% of the cakes from Bakery B are not baked properly either.

Mr M has just bought a new cake, which is not baked properly. What is the probability that that cake was made in Bakery B? (2 d.p.)

```

```

211 RECYC

Recyc plc is a company which reprocesses factory waste in order to extract good quality aluminium. Information concerning its operations is as follows:

1   Recyc plc places an advance order each year for chemical X for use in the aluminium extraction process. It will enter into an advance contract for the coming year for chemical X at one of three levels – high, medium or low, which correspond to the requirements of a high, medium or low level of waste available for reprocessing.

2   The level of waste available will not be known when the advance order for chemical X is entered into. A set of probabilities have been estimated by management as to the likelihood of the quantity of waste being at a high, medium or low level.

3   Where the advance order entered into for chemical X is lower than that required for the level of waste for processing actually received, a discount from the original demand price is allowed by the supplier for the total quantity of chemical X actually required.

4   Where the advance order entered into for chemical X is in excess of that required to satisfy the actual level of waste for reprocessing, a penalty payment in excess of the original demand price is payable for the total quantity of chemical X actually required.

A summary of the information relating to the above points is as follows:

				Chemical X costs per kg	
Level of reprocessing	**Waste available**	**Probability**	**Advance order**	**Conversion discount**	**Conversion premium**
	000 kg		$	$	$
High	50,000	0.30	1.00		
Medium	38,000	0.50	1.20		
Low	30,000	0.20	1.40		
Chemical X: order conversion:					
Low to medium				0.10	
Medium to high				0.10	
Low to high				0.15	
Medium to low					0.25
High to medium					0.25
High to low					0.60

Aluminium is sold at $0.65 per kg. Variable costs (excluding chemical X costs) are 70% of sales revenue. Aluminium extracted from the waste is 15% of the waste input. Chemical X is added to the reprocessing at the rate of 1 kg per 100 kg of waste.

Complete a summary which shows the budgeted contribution earned by Recyc plc for the coming year for each of nine possible outcomes:

		Level of waste		
		High	**Medium**	**Low**
Advance order of chemical	High			
	Medium			
	Low			

State the contribution for the coming year which corresponds to the use of:

(i)   maximax

$ [   ]

and

(ii)   maximin decision criteria.

$ [   ]

212   TICKET AGENT

A ticket agent has an arrangement with a concert hall that holds concerts on 60 nights a year whereby they receive discounts as follows per concert:

For purchase of:	receive a discount of:
200 tickets	20%
300 tickets	25%
400 tickets	30%
500 tickets or more	40%

Purchases must be in full hundreds. The average price per ticket is $30.

The ticket agent must decide in advance each year the number of tickets they will purchase. If they have any tickets unsold by the afternoon of the concert, they must return them to the box office. If the box office sells any of these, the ticket agent receives 60% of their price.

The ticket agent's sales records over a few years show that for a concert with extremely popular artistes, they can be confident of selling 500 tickets, for one with lesser known artistes; 350 tickets, and for one with relatively unknown artistes; 200 tickets.

Past data shows that 10% of the tickets returned are sold by the box office. (**Note:** These are in addition to any sales made by the ticket agent).

Administration costs incurred in selling tickets are the same per concert irrespective of the popularity of the artistes.

Sales records show that the frequency of concerts will be:

With popular artistes	45%
With lesser known artistes	30%
With unknown artistes	25%
	———
	100%
	———

Calculate the expected demand for tickets per concert:

Calculate the level of purchases of tickets per concert that will give the ticket agent the largest profit over a long period of time:

Calculate the profit per concert that this level of purchases of tickets will yield:

$

Calculate the number of tickets the agent should buy, based on the following criteria:

Maximin

Maximax

Minimax regret

213 SHIFTERS HAULAGE

Shifters Haulage (SH) is considering changing some of the vans it uses to transport crates for customers. The new vans come in three sizes; small, medium and large. SH is unsure about which type to buy. The capacity is 100 crates for the small van, 150 for the medium van and 200 for the large van. Demand for crates varies and can be either 120 or 190 crates per period, with the probability of the higher demand figure being 0.6.

The sale price per crate is $10 and the variable cost $4 per crate for all van sizes subject to the fact that if the capacity of the van is greater than the demand for crates in a period then the variable cost will be lower by 10% to allow for the fact that the vans will be partly empty when transporting crates.

SH is concerned that if the demand for crates exceeds the capacity of the vans then customers will have to be turned away. SH estimates that in this case goodwill of $100 would be charged against profits per period to allow for lost future sales regardless of the number of customers that are turned away.

Depreciation charged would be $200 per period for the small, $300 for the medium and $400 for the large van.

SH has in the past been very aggressive in its decision-making, pressing ahead with rapid growth strategies. However, its managers have recently grown more cautious as the business has become more competitive.

Complete a profits table showing the SIX possible profit figures per period.

214 COOL SYSTEMS

Cool Systems, a producer of air conditioning systems for customers in the building trade, is having some problems with the manufacturing process for a particular system, the Breeze. Under its current production process, 25% of the Breeze units are defective. The unit contribution of this system is $40 per unit. Under contract the company has with its customers, Cool systems refunds $60 for each 'Breeze' that the customer finds to be defective; the customers then repair the system to make it usable in their building work.

Before delivering the systems to customers, Cool Systems could spend an additional $30 per Breeze to rework any systems thought to be defective – regardless of whether the system really is defective. The reworked systems can be sold at the regular price and will definitely not be defective in the builders' projects. Unfortunately, Cool Systems cannot tell ahead of time which systems will fail to work in their builders' installations, but would not deliver a system where tests had revealed a problem.

The summary table that shows the budgeted contribution per unit earned by Cool Systems for each of the possible 4 outcomes has been correctly prepared as follows:

	Breeze system is not defective	Breeze system is defective
Cool Systems chooses to rework	$40 – $30 = $10	$40 – $30 = $10
Cool Systems chooses NOT to rework	$40	$40 – $60 = ($20)

A consultant engineer has developed a simple test device to evaluate the system before delivering. For each system, the test device registers positive (i.e. no problem), inconclusive or negative. The test is not perfect, but it is consistent for a particular system; this means the test yields the same result for a given system regardless of how many times it is tested.

To calibrate the test device, it was run on a sample batch of 100 systems. The results are presented in the table below:

	System in good condition: 75 systems in total	System in defective condition: 25 systems in total
Test result : Positive	52.5 systems	2.5 systems
Test result : Inconclusive	15 systems	7.5 systems
Test result : Negative	7.5 systems	15 systems

What is the maximum (per system) the company should be willing to pay for using the test device? Use a decision tree approach to calculate your answer.

$ [   ]

215   THEATRE

A theatre has a seating capacity of 500 people and is considering engaging MS and her orchestra for a concert for one night only. The fee that would be charged by MS would be $10,000. If the theatre engages MS, then this sum is payable regardless of the size of the theatre audience.

Based on past experience of events of this type, the price of the theatre ticket would be $25 per person. The size of the audience for this event is uncertain, but based on past experience it is expected to be as follows:

	Probability
300 people	50%
400 people	30%
500 people	20%

In addition to the sale of the theatre tickets, it can be expected that members of the audience will also purchase confectionery both prior to the performance and during the interval. The contribution that this would yield to the theatre is unclear, but has been estimated as follows:

Contribution from confectionery sales	Probability
Contribution of $3 per person	30%
Contribution of $5 per person	50%
Contribution of $10 per person	20%

What is the expected value of profits if MS is engaged for the concert?

$ _____

Prepare a two-way data table to show the profit values that could occur from deciding to engage MS for the concert:

Confectionary sales / Ticket sales	$3 per person	$5 per person	$10 per person
300 people			
400 people			
500 people			

216 AMELIE

Amelie is setting up in business importing French cheeses. She could open up a small shop, a large outlet, or no shop at all if she decides to sell online only (which she won't be able to do for another few years at least).

There will be a 5 year lease on a few shops currently available in the centre of town, and Amelie wants to make the correct decision.

Amelie is also thinking about hiring a consultant to conduct a market research study. If the study is conducted, the results could indicate that the cheese market is either favourable or unfavourable.

Amelie believes there is a 50-50 chance that the market will be favourable, and expects her profits to be as follows if she opens her shop:

	Favourable market	Unfavourable market
Large shop	$60,000	($40,000) loss
Small shop	$30,000	($10,000) loss

The consultant has quoted a charge of $5,000 for the marketing research. They have also hinted that there is a 0.6 probability that the survey will indicate that the cheese market would be favourable.

There is a 0.9 probability that the cheese market will be favourable given a favourable outcome from the study.

The consultant warned Amelie that there is only a probability of 0.12 of a favourable market if the marketing research results are not favourable. Amelie is confused.

A decision tree for Amelie has correctly been drawn as follows to explain whether Amelie should hire the market research consultant:

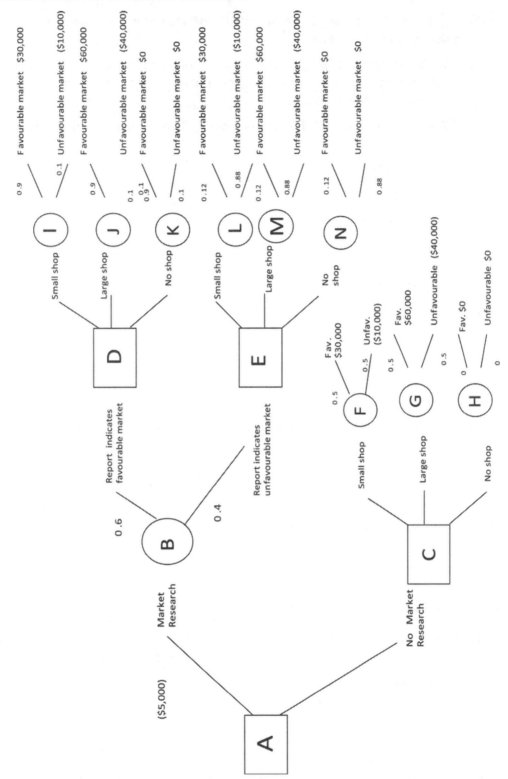

After discussing the competence of the consultant with another business owner, Amelie now believes that she'd rather contact another market research company which guarantees perfect information concerning the cheese market profitability.

Calculate the value of this perfect information.

217 **Which of the following statements regarding risk and uncertainty in decision making is/are true?**

(1)   Decision trees can be used to generate perfect information relating to a sequence of decisions and outcomes.

(2)   Simulation models assign probability distributions to large numbers of project variables and use random number generators to estimate a probability distribution of outcomes for the project.

(3)   The maximax approach to decision making is best suited to risk-seeking decision-makers.

A   (1), (2) and (3)

B   (1) and (3) only

C   (2) and (3) only

D   (2) only

218 **Which concept is not part of the 3Vs of Big Data?**

A   Volume

B   Variety

C   Valorisation

D   Velocity

219 **Complete the following text by selecting the missing words and phrases (the same word may be used more than once):**

external	gather	analyse	traditional
websites	unstructured	social networks	planning
insights	customer demand	structured	systems
	customer experience	features	

Big Data management involves using sophisticated _____ to _____, store and _____ large volumes of data in a variety of _____ and _____ formats. In addition to _____ data from internal sources such as sales history, preferences, order frequency and pricing information, companies can also gather information from _____ sources such as _____, trade publications and _____.

Collating and analysing these large volumes of information allows companies to gain a variety of _____ into customer behaviour and this can help to more accurately predict _____.

These demand forecasts may be in terms of volume but also the type of products required and this is beneficial to company _____ but can also help the company to improve aspects of the _____. In terms of volume predictions, these can help to ensure that a company will always have sufficient inventory to satisfy demand. This will mean that customers do not need to wait to receive their goods which is likely to be a key part of their shopping experience. Furthermore companies can use the information and _____ to understand which products and _____ are most popular with customers. This can inform product re-design to ensure that any revisions are in line with customer preferences.

220 **Complete the following text by selecting the missing words and phrases (the same word may be used more than once):**

volume	storage	useful	traditional
websites	data	social networks	sources
insights	wasted	variety	systems
standard	velocity	features	e-commerce

Business data can be difficult to manage for a variety of reasons and these can be summarised using the 3 V's of velocity, volume and variety.

- The first 'V is '_____': the speed at which data is now generated from sources such as social media networks makes it incredibly difficult for _____ database management systems to cope and give relevant and timely _____. If this_____ is not managed effectively it is, at best, _____ but could also result in significant increases in the data _____ capacity required, without seeing any particular benefits.

- The second 'V is '_____': Companies can now gather and generate data from a huge range of _____ including internal systems, _____ sources, competitor and customer websites and social media networks. Not only has the overall _____ of sources increased but the amount of data gathered from each source is now much higher than from _____ reporting. For example the data gathered from a single e-commerce sales transaction can be up to ten times higher than a _____ in-store transaction. It is important that data is only gathered (and therefore stored and analysed) from relevant _____ that can actually add value to company decision making as there is a danger that companies become obsessed with gathering all data that is available rather than just that which is _____.

- The third 'V is '_____': An increasing number of incompatible and inconsistent data formats is emerging at a fast rate. Most traditional data management _____ are based around extracting data from, and storing data in, standard formats such as XML. Collecting data in a wide variety of formats including sound files and GPS data creates challenges for a system managing such big data.

221 A business is faced with a risk that has a low probability of occurring and a high negative impact if it does occur, but the related activity cannot be avoided because it is strategically vital to undertake for the business.

Which of the following strategies is likely to be best suited to dealing with this risk?

A   Transfer

B   Avoid

C   Reduce

D   Accept

222 A business is faced with a risk that has a high probability of occurring and a high negative impact if it does occur. It is not strategically vital for the business to undertake the activity.

Which of the following strategies is likely to be best suited to dealing with this risk?

A   Transfer

B   Avoid

C   Reduce

D   Accept

223 A business is faced with a risk that has a low probability of occurring and a low negative impact if it does occur. The risk is not really a matter, even if it is realised.

Which of the following strategies is likely to be best suited to dealing with this risk?

A   Transfer

B   Avoid

C   Reduce

D   Accept

224 A business is faced with a risk that has a high probability of occurring and a low negative impact if it does occur. The business is thinking about using a different method to carry out the activity.

Which of the following strategies is likely to be best suited to dealing with this risk?

A   Transfer

B   Avoid

C   Reduce

D   Accept

225 In a group of 100 CIMA students, 30 are male, 55 are studying for Certificate Stage and 6 of the male students are not studying for Certificate Stage. A student chosen at random is female.

What is the probability that she is not studying Certificate Stage?

A   0.80

B   0.56

C   0.44

D   0.20

226   Mail order buyers of Brand X classified by area and age (years)

Age	Under 25	25–44	45–64	65 +
Area				
North	400	350	300	250
South	600	550	500	450
East	200	150	100	50
West	400	350	300	250
Totals	1,600	1,400	1,200	1,000

Calculate:

The probability that a randomly-selected brand X buyer is from the north and under 25 years of age is (to 2 decimal places):

P = [   ]

The probability that a randomly-selected Brand X buyer is from the West or under 25 years of age is (to 2 decimal places):

P = [   ]

The probability that a randomly-selected Brand X buyer, who is under 25 years of age, is from the South is (to 3 decimal places):

P = [   ]

The probability that two randomly-selected Brand X buyers are both under 25 years of age is (to two decimal places):

P = [   ]

Section 2

ANSWERS TO OBJECTIVE TEST QUESTIONS

A: MANAGING THE COSTS OF CREATING VALUE

1   B

	E	F	G	Total
Budgeted number of batches to be produced:	75,000/200	120,000/60	60,000/30	
	= 375	= 2,000	= 2,000	
Machine set-ups per batch:	5	3	9	
Total machine set-ups	1,875	6,000	18,000	25,875

So budgeted cost per set-up: $180,000/25,875 = $6.96 per set-up

Therefore the budgeted machine set-up cost per unit of F produced is:

($6.96 × 3)/60 = $0.35 per unit or $6.96 × 6,000/120,000 = $0.35 per unit

2   B, C and E

Traditional costing systems assume that products consume activities in proportion to their production volumes, which means that high-volume products absorb too much overhead and low-volume products too little. ABC remedies this by absorbing overheads based on the actual use each product makes of the overhead activities. ABC still provides historic information on product costs but it can be viewed as the best estimate of longer term product costs as in the long term all costs are variable. It therefore supports longer-term strategic decision making in areas such as product pricing, product range and mix, and new product development.

3   A

Since all of the activities listed are directly related to the goods that are sold in the supermarket, DPP (based on ABC) requires that all of the costs should be included in the calculation.

4   B

Pareto analysis is a cumulative analysis, taking the items in descending order of size. Here, the products should be in descending order of total sales revenue earned.

Product	Sales revenue
	$
D	100,000
A	50,000
B	40,000
C	30,000
E	20,000
	_____
	240,000
	_____

5   (i)   Set ups

1 for every 10 units of A, 1 for every 10 units of B, 1 per day for C = 50 + 40 + 20 = 110

Charge out rate = \$2,200/110 = \$20 per driver

Total charge to C = 20 × \$20 = \$400

Cost per unit for C = \$400/20 = \$20

(ii)   Inspections

Ratio is 1:1:2 = 500 + 400 + 40 = 940

Charge out rate = \$2,820/940 = \$3 per driver

Total charge to C= 40 × \$3 = \$120

Cost per unit for C = \$120/20 = \$6

So total cost per unit for C = \$26.00

6   B

7   All statements apply.

First, the results are rearranged in descending order of contribution and a cumulative contribution figure calculated.

Product	Contribution	Cumulative contribution	Cumulative
	$(000)	$(000)	%
White loaves	94	94	25
Individual cakes	83	177	46
Brown loaves	67	244	64
Family-sized cakes	53	297	78
Plain rolls	42	339	89
Filled rolls	26	365	96
Pasties and pies	16	381	100
	____		
	381		
	____		

The cumulative data can now be used to produce the required Pareto chart showing product contribution:

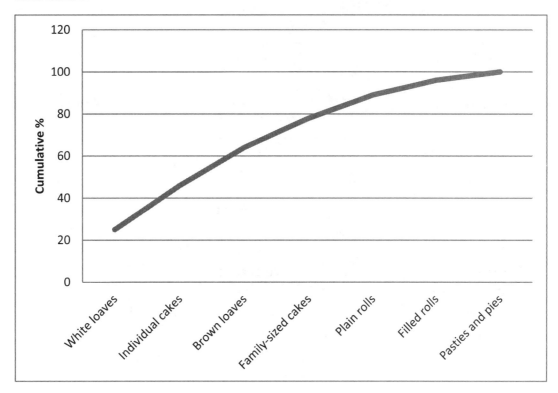

It is clear from the diagram that four of the product lines make up nearly 80% of the contribution for the bakery firm.

The most popular products are bread and cakes and with white loaves outselling all other products. Management attention should be focused on these areas.

8   A cost <u>driver</u> is any <u>factor</u> that causes a change in the <u>cost</u> of an <u>activity</u>, so the most important factor when selecting a <u>cost</u> driver is to identify a **causal** relationship between the cost driver and the costs. Such a relationship may arise because of some physical relationship or because of the logic of the situation.

For example, <u>quality inspection</u> costs are caused by the action of carrying out an inspection to ensure quality <u>standards</u> are being achieved, so the appropriate cost <u>driver</u> would be the number of <u>inspections</u> carried out. Some <u>activities</u> may have <u>multiple</u> cost drivers associated with them; in such a situation it is best if the costs can be analysed into separate <u>cost pools</u> for each of which a <u>single</u> driver can be identified.

9   X PLC

Power: | $12,575 | per KJ

Stores: | $3,776 | per order

Maintenance: | $2,246 | per machine hour

Machinery cleaning: | $2,439 | per set-up

The budgeted costs are:

Activity	Total	Appropriate cost driver
	$000	
Power	1,250	Power (kj) per batch
Stores	1,850	Purchase orders per batch
Maintenance	2,100	Machine hours per batch
Machinery cleaning	800	Machine set-ups per batch
Indirect labour	1,460	Standard labour hours per batch

For each activity we must calculate a cost driver rate.

Power

Total budgeted power = $(1.4 \times 36) + (1.7 \times 10) + (0.8 \times 40)$

= 99.4 kj

$\therefore$ Cost driver rate $= \dfrac{\$1.25m}{99.4}$ = $12,575 per kj

Stores

Total budgeted purchase orders = $(5 \times 36) + (3 \times 10) + (7 \times 40)$

= 490 orders

$\therefore$ Cost driver rate $= \dfrac{\$1.85m}{490}$ = $3,776 per order

Maintenance

Total budgeted machine hours = $(10 \times 36) + (7.5 \times 10) + (12.5 \times 40) = 935$ hours

$\therefore$ Cost driver rate $= \dfrac{\$2.1m}{935}$ = $2,246 per machine hour

Machinery cleaning

Total budgeted machine set-ups = $(3 \times 36) + (2 \times 10) + (5 \times 40)$

= 328 set-ups

$\therefore$ Cost driver rate $= \dfrac{\$0.8m}{328}$ = $2,439 per set-up

10   Overheads absorbed on machine hour basis

Machine hour absorption rate = Total overheads/Total machine hours

$$= \frac{\$10,430 + \$5,250 + \$3,600 + \$2,100 + \$4,620}{(120 \times 4) + (100 \times 3) + (80 \times 2) + (120 \times 3)} = \frac{\$26,000}{1,300} = \$20 \text{ per machine hour}$$

	Total costs in $
Product A	$17,760
Product B	$13,100
Product C	$6,720
Product D	$16,920

Workings – Total costs based on machine hour basis

	A	B	C	D
	$	$	$	$
Direct materials	40	50	30	60
Direct labour	28	21	14	21
Production overhead	80	60	40	60
Production cost/unit	**148**	**131**	**841**	**141**
Output in units	120	100	80	120
Total production cost	**$17,760**	**$13,100**	**$6,720**	**$16,920**

Overheads absorbed based on ABC

	Total costs in $
Product A	$16,331
Product B	$13,257
Product C	$7,984
Product D	$16,928

	Overhead costs		
	$	**Level of activity**	**Cost/activity**
Machine department cost	10,430	1,300	$8.02/hour
Set-up costs	5,250	21*	$250.00/run
Stores receiving costs	3,600	80**	$45.00/requisition
Inspection/quality costs	2,100	21*	$100.00/run
Material handling and despatch	4,620	42	$110.00/order

Workings

*No of production runs   = output in units/20

$$= \frac{120 + 100 + 80 + 120}{20}$$

$$= \frac{420}{20} = 21$$

**No of requisition raised   = No. of products × 20

= 4 × 20 = 80

Total costs based on ABC

	A	B	C	D
	$	$	$	$
Direct materials	40.00	50.00	30.00	60.00
Direct labour	28.00	21.00	14.00	21.00
Machine dept costs	32.09	24.07	16.05	24.07
Set-up costs	12.50	12.50	12.50	12.50
Stores receiving	7.50	9.00	11.25	7.50
Inspection	5.00	5.00	5.00	5.00
Material handling	11.00	11.00	11.00	11.00
Production cost/unit	**136.09**	**132.57**	**99.80**	**141.07**
Output in units	120	100	80	120
Total production costs	**$16,331**	**$13,257**	**$7,984**	**$16,928**

11 D

In target costing, the selling price of a product is determined first and the target costs established accordingly.

12 C

External failure costs are those incurred due to poor quality of goods delivered to customers; therefore this includes compensation costs.

Appraisal costs are those incurred in the measuring of quality of output; therefore this includes test equipment running costs.

13 B

Machine cells, multi-skilled labour and a close relationship with suppliers are all features of JIT. A focus on inventory being held at a bottleneck resource is a feature of throughput accounting.

14 D

Statements A, B and C are incorrect. JIT makes an organisation more vulnerable to disruptions in the supply chain because there are no buffer inventories as protection against a breakdown in supply. JIT is easier to implement when an organisation operates within a narrow geographical area, and close to its suppliers. (At Toyota, where JIT originated, manufacturing operations were initially carried out within a 50 kilometre radius.) With little or no inventories, the risk of inventory obsolescence should not exist.

Statement D is correct. When demand is difficult to predict, it becomes more difficult to operate a demand-driven operation.

15 B

(i) is true. JIT is a 'pull' system, based on demand. (ii) is false : while a low batch set-up costs are a prerequisite for successful JIT, the use of JIT will result in smaller batches, more set-ups and hence higher set up costs overall. (iii) is true. JIT needs multifunctional workers, who could be grouped by products rather than tasks.

16 D

Product return per minute = (selling price – direct material cost)/time on bottleneck resource
= \$(45 – 14)/10 = \$3.10

17 D

	J	K	L	M
	\$	\$	\$	\$
Selling price	2,000	1,500	1,500	1,750
Direct materials	410	200	300	400
Throughput	1,590	1,300	1,200	1,350
Minutes on Machine X	120	100	70	110
Throughput per minute	\$13.25	\$13.00	\$17.14	\$12.27
Ranking	2	3	1	4

18 B

	\$
Sales revenue: 600 units × \$450	270,000
Return on investment required: 20% × \$300,000	60,000
Total cost allowed	210,000
Target cost per unit: 210,000/600	350

19 Processing 70 units of product T will give the larger throughput contribution per day.

	Product S	Product T
Throughput of process X per day	$13.5 \text{ hrs} \times \frac{60}{5} = 162.00$	$13.5 \text{ hrs} \times \frac{60}{7.5} = 108.00$

(Production time: 15 – 1.5 = 13.5 hrs)

	Product S	Product T
Throughput of process Y per day	$14 \text{ hrs} \times \frac{60}{18} = 46.67$	$14 \text{ hrs} \times \frac{60}{12} = 70.00$

(Production time : 15 – 1 = 14 hrs)

Process Y limits the production of both products to figures that are less than sales demand.

Throughput contribution per hour of product S: $\frac{(\$95.00 - 20.00)}{18} \times 60 = \$250.00$

Throughput contribution per hour of product T: $\frac{(\$85.00 - 20.00)}{12} \times 60 = \$325.00$

SUBJECT P2 : ADVANCED MANAGEMENT ACCOUNTING

20

Statements	True	False
Throughput contribution per hour is likely to be reduced.		✓
The differences between marginal and absorption costing profit will be reduced.	✓	

JIT employs more flexible production systems which typically reduce the time spent on the throughput bottleneck. This will increase the throughput contribution per hour.

As there will be lower inventory in a JIT system and the difference between marginal and absorption costing profit is caused by differences in the valuation of inventory, a switch to JIT will reduce the differences between marginal and absorption costing profit.

21 D

TQM can be applied to any type of organisation and not just manufacturers.. The other statements are true.

22 D

	J	H	K
	$	$	$
Gross margin	2,000,000	3,000,000	2,500,000
Sales visits at $400	62,400	68,800	83,200
Order processing at $50	75,000	75,000	100,000
Despatch at $150	225,000	225,000	300,000
Billing and collection at $150	450,000	450,000	600,000
Total	812,400	818,800	1,083,200
Net profit/(loss) per customer	1,187,600	2,181,200	1,416,800
Ranking	3	1	2

23   D

It is worth noting that the labour cost is not needed here: it is a direct cost and will not change, regardless of the method used. We will calculate the overhead cost per unit under both systems and calculate the difference.

AC: since the time per unit is the same for each product, the overheads per unit will also be the same.

$156,000/6,000 units = $26 (we would get the same answer using labour hours)

ABC:	Number of deliveries for X	1,000/200	= 5
	Number of deliveries for Y	2,000/400	= 5
	Number of deliveries for Z	3,000/1,000	= 3
	Total		= 13

Cost per delivery $156,000/13 = $12,000

Cost per unit of Z: ($12,000 per deliver × 3 deliveries)/(Total units required 3,000 units) = $12

Decrease $26 – $12 = $14

24   TPAR = 1.50

The return per factory hour = ($100 – $40)/3.75 hours = $16

Factory costs per factory hour = ($10 + $30)/3.75 hours = $10.67

Throughput accounting ratio = Return per factory hour/cost per factory hour
= $16/$10.67 = 1.50.

25   C

Unit, batch, product and facility all relate to levels of activity, while value added and non-value added relate to the type of activity.

26   C

Statement (i) provides a definition of a cost driver. Cost drivers for long-term variable overhead costs will be the volume of a particular activity to which the cost driver relates, so Statement (ii) is correct. Statement (iii) is also correct. In traditional absorption costing, standard high-volume products receive a higher amount of overhead costs than with ABC. ABC allows for the unusually high costs of support activities for low-volume products (such as relatively higher set-up costs, order processing costs and so on).

27 The answer is $7.50

Number of batches per product given by total production units/batch size

Product X   number of batches = 15/2.5 = 6
Product Y   number of batches = 25/5 = 5
Product Z   number of batches = 20/4 = 5

Total number of batches = 16

Machine set up costs attributed to products in same ratio as number of batches

Set up costs for product Y = 5/16 × $600,000 = $187,500

Since there are 25,000 units of Y in total, the machine set-up costs that would be attributed to each unit of Product Y is $187,500/25,000 units = $7.50.

28 A

Cost	Classification
(i)	Facility-sustaining
(ii)	Facility-sustaining
(iii)	Product-sustaining
(iv)	Product-sustaining
(v)	Facility-sustaining

29

Washing	1,200 × (60/6)	=	12,000 units
Filling	700 × (60/3)	=	14,000 units
Capping	250 × (60/1.5)	=	10,000 units
Labelling	450 × (60/2)	=	13,500 units
Packing	1,300 × (60/6)	=	13,000 units

Maximum output is therefore limited by the capping process to 10,000 units.

Throughput per unit	=	$0.60 – $0.18	=	$0.42
Time on bottleneck	=	1.5/60	=	0.025 of an hour
Return per hour	=	$0.42/0.025	=	$16.80
Total factory cost	=	$4,120 + $0.02 × 10,000	=	$4,320
Cost per hour	=	$4,320/250 hours	=	$17.28 per hr
TA ratio	=	16.80/17.28	=	0.97

30 All are true. Since quality is customer defined, everyone should become customer focused. Standard costing implies that there is a standard that is good enough, TQM is based on continuous improvement. Last, quality control departments are believed to reinforce the idea that quality is someone else's problem; With TQM, quality is incorporated in everyone's targets.

31   Purchasing costs will increase due to the extra requirements applied to suppliers. Stockholding costs will reduce due to lower stock levels. Ordering costs will increase due to the greater specification required, and the increased number of small deliveries. Switching from a traditional inventory ordering system to a just-in-time ordering system would result in increased information system costs in the short term at least, because of implementation, training and upgrade costs of the systems.

32   **C**

A is not correct: unless there is a quality programme of some type, a company cannot afford to have low stocks, in case defective items need to be replaced from stock. B is not rue either: whilst TQM can be used by service companies, it is also seen in manufacturing and other productive industries along with JIT. Statement C is closely related to the truth; customer satisfaction as regards quality and delivery times. D is not right because a TQM system is more concerned with ensuring that errors do not occur in the first place. Any checking of items can be undertaken during the production process itself.

33   **A**

The resale value is normally referred to as the 'exchange value'.

34   **A**

Batch production uses stocks to supply customers whilst other products are being produced. Stocks are avoided in a JIT system. **Jobbing production** makes products to customer order and is ideal for JIT. **Process production** produces continuous output, and as long as the speed of production can be regulated, this can be tailored to customer requirements. **Services** are always produced just in time, as they cannot be stored.

35   **B**

(i) should help to prevent failures. (ii) is the cost of a quality failure discovered externally (it has been returned). (iii) represents appraising the current production and (iv) is the cost of a quality failure discovered internally.

36   Value analysis is an examination of the <u>factors</u> affecting the cost of a product or service with the objective of achieving the specified purpose most <u>economically</u> at the required level of <u>quality</u> and <u>reliability</u>.

<u>Functional</u> analysis is an analysis of the <u>relationships</u> between product functions, the <u>cost</u> of their provision and their perceived <u>value</u> to the customer.

Therefore, <u>value</u> analysis is a form of cost <u>reduction</u> which is based upon investigating the processes involved in providing a product or service, whereas <u>functional</u> analysis focuses on the value to the customer of each <u>function</u> of the product or service and from this determines whether it is necessary to reduce the cost of providing each function.

37   **B**

38 D

JIT typically requires changes in how materials are requisitioned for production and a change in production in staffing to make them more flexible. But finished goods will likely be delivered in the same way (though the timing and quantity may change).

39 Just-in-Time, like so many modern management techniques, places great importance on the 'continuous improvement' ethos. Cost containment will often aim to achieve a pre-determined target, but this target may often remain static over a long period of time. With modern techniques, the target is regularly updated and made more stringent.

Continual cost reduction can be seen in many areas of JIT:

- Reduction in stock levels – large amounts of capital is tied up in high stock levels. Reducing stock levels releases this cash, so that it can be better used elsewhere in the business. Ideally, zero stock should be held.

- Reduction in manufacturing times and customer lead times – the demand based manufacturing of JIT, together with cellular manufacturing enables production times to be greatly reduced. This will improve customer satisfaction and hopefully lead to increased business volume.

- Cross-training of staff: new production methods necessitate staff being competent in several tasks. This may lead to fewer staff being required hence costs are reduced.

40

Costs associated with stopping the output of products which fail to conform to the specifications. **Prevention costs.**	Costs of materials or products that fail to meet specifications. **Internal failure costs.**
Costs arising when poor quality products are delivered to customers. **External failure costs.**	Costs associated with ensuring that production meets standards. **Appraisal costs.**

41 TPAR = 1.3

The throughput accounting ratio is defined as throughput/total factory costs. Throughput accounting aims to discourage inventory building, so the ratios do not take account of inventory movements.

Throughput = sales – all material costs =$35 × 800 – $13,000 = $15,000

(Note that we use materials purchased instead of materials used.)

Total factory costs = all other production costs = $6,900 + $4,650 = $11,550

TA ratio = $15,000/$11,550 = 1.30.

42 D

43   **B**

44   The extended value <u>chain</u> includes both <u>internal</u> and external <u>factors</u> whereas the <u>value chain</u> includes only the internal factors. The value chain is the <u>sequence</u> of business <u>factors</u> that add <u>value</u> to the organisation's <u>products</u> and services and comprises the following:

- Research and Development (R&D)

- Design

- Production

- Marketing

- <u>Distribution</u>

- Customer service

The extended value chain adds <u>suppliers</u> to the left hand side and <u>customers</u> to the right hand side and recognises the importance of the <u>relationships</u> that the organisation has with these external parties in the overall process of adding value.

45   **C**

$$\text{Lifecycle cost of new product in Skipping Co} = \frac{\text{Total Costs of product over its entire lifecycle (3 years)}}{\text{Total number of units}}$$

	Year 1	Year 2	Year 3
Units made and sold: 14,000 in total	3,000	6,000	5,000
	$	$	$
Design costs	2,000	500	500
Total variable production cost: Unit variable production cost × number of units made	45,600	88,800	72,500
Fixed production costs	2,700	2,800	2,900
Total variable production cost: Unit variable production cost × number of units sold	2,400	5,400	4,750
Distribution and customer service costs	2,000	3,500	2,500
Total costs	54,700	101,000	83,150

$$\text{Lifecycle cost of new product in Skipping Co} = \frac{\$54,700 + \$101,000 + \$83,150}{14,000 \text{ units}} = \$17.06 \text{ per unit}$$

46   **D**

A product's life cycle costs are very inclusive; none of these would be excluded.

B: CAPITAL INVESTMENT DECISION-MAKING

47   X PLC

$4,900

100 reams @ resale value of $10	$1,000
150 reams @ market price of $26	$3,900
	————
	$4,900
	————

48   The maximum amount that the company should be prepared to pay an external supplier is $114,000 ($22.80 per unit) and to cover its own cost, the business must produce 215 units, to the nearest.

This question is testing the 'make or buy' decision. The business should choose to do whichever is the cheaper of the two options.

If component D12 is purchased from an external supplier, the maximum it should be prepared to pay is equal to the cost it would incur in making the component itself.

Making component D12 itself cost the business $21.00 per unit (this being the marginal cost of making each unit). If the component were not manufactured in-house the avoidable fixed costs of $9,000 would not be incurred.

So cost of manufacturing 5,000 units of D12 = $9,000 + $21.00 × 5,000 = $114,000.

This is therefore the maximum amount that the company should be prepared to pay an external supplier.

If the component D12 is bought-in at a cost of $25 per unit, the contribution made by the business from each unit if F45 sold will be:

	$
Selling price	146
Less:	
Variable costs (includes the $25 for component D12)	(62)
	————
Contribution	84
	————

The avoidable fixed costs associated with making F45 are $18,000.

(The question asked for the number of units of product F45 that must be sold to cover its own costs without contributing to T plc's non-avoidable fixed costs, that is, to cover the avoidable fixed costs only.)

To cover this cost the business must produce the following number of units of F45:

$18,000/$84 = 214.29 units. So, 215 units to the nearest.

49   E

By setting up your own business you will be giving up the **opportunity** to earn $25,000 per annum. The salary is therefore an opportunity cost. By taking on the rent of the business unit you will be increasing your cost base – so the rent is an incremental cost.

A committed cost is a cost which the new business is already obliged to pay (perhaps for contractual reasons). Sunk costs are past costs. Irrelevant costs are those that have no bearing on the decision to be taken.

50   RIGHTLIGHT LTD

If the contract were to go ahead, five new employees will have to be recruited at an incremental cost of 5 × $45,000 = $225,000 per annum.

This cost would only be for six months.

So cost to the contract would be: $225,000 × 0.5 = $112,500

The cost of the project manager is irrelevant since they already work for Rightlight Ltd. Their salary is therefore a committed cost – even the 30% of time they will spend on the contract!

The 'Environmental Awareness' training programme would cost:

5 employees × $3,000 × 80% = $12,000

So total relevant cost if Rightlight Ltd were to run the campaign would be:

$112,500 + $12,000 = $124,500

Instead, Rightlight Ltd could subcontract the work at a cost of $135,000.

The cheaper option is to employ and train the five new employees. Hence, relevant cost of labour for the contract is $124,500.

51

Cost or benefit	Quantitative cost	Quantitative benefit	Qualitative cost	Qualitative benefit
The impact on employee morale of adding a common room with tea and coffee facilities in the production area				✓
Reduction in sales teams travelling expenses after moving all account management activities to Internet-based support solutions		✓		
Increase in market share		✓		
Lower employee morale and productivity linked to pay cuts			✓	
More recognised corporate branding				✓

Cost or benefit	Quantitative cost	Quantitative benefit	Qualitative cost	Qualitative benefit
The impact on the community of allowing employees to spend a few hours of paid time assisting local charities				✓
Advertising investment in e-commerce sites and social media platforms	✓			

52   C

	$	Tax saved at 25%	Yr 1	Yr 2	Yr 3
Cost of asset	80,000				
Year 1 writing down allowance (20%)	16,000	4,000	2,000	2,000	
Balance	64,000				
Year 2 writing down allowance (20%)	12,800	3,200		1,600	1,600
				———	
				3,600	

Cash flows in the second year

	$
Tax relief on asset	3,600
Cash inflow	25,000
Tax due – year 1 cash flow $25,000 × 25% × 0.5	(3,125)
Tax due – year 2 cash flow $25,000 × 25% × 0.5	(3,125)
	22,350
Discount factor, year 2 at 5%	0.907
Present value of cash flows in Year 2	$20,271

53   B, C and E

There are three main reasons for the time value of money:

There is a strong preference for the immediate rather than delayed consumption. It is always preferable to take the money now because it could be invested to earn interest.

In most countries, in most years, prices rise as a result of inflation. Therefore funds received today will buy more than the same amount a year later, as prices will have risen in the meantime.

The earlier cash flows are due to be received, the more certain they are – there is less chance that events will prevent payment.

It is true that reported annual profits are subjective. It is also true that operating costs tend to rise due to deteriorating machinery. However neither are reasons for the time value of money.

54   A

Annual cost of capital: 10%

Inflation rate: 4%

Real rate: (1.10/1.04) − 1 = 0.0577

Year 1 discount rate:	1/1.0577	0.945
Year 2 discount rate:	$1/(1.0577^2)$	0.894
Year 3 discount rate:	$1/(1.0577^3)$	0.845
Year 4 discount rate:	$1/(1.0577^4)$	0.799
		─────
		3.483
		─────

Annual inflow years 1–4: 6,000 × $12 = $72,000

			Discount rate	$
Year 0	Investment	$250,000	0	250,000
Year 1–4	Inflow	$72,000	3.483	250,776
				─────
	NPV			$776 i.e. $800
				─────

Alternatively, you can reach the same solution (with some differences possibly for rounding error) by inflating all the cash flows at 4% to their 'out-turn' amount, and discounting these inflated cash flows at the money cost of capital, 10%. The cash flows would be ($72,000 × 1.04) $74,880 in year 1, $77,875 in year 2, $80,990 in year 3 and $84,230 in year 4.

55   B

Year	Cash inflow/(outflow)	Discount factor @ 8%	Present value $
0	(60,000)	1.000	(60,000)
1	23,350	0.926	21,622
2	29,100	0.857	24,939
3	27,800	0.794	22,073
			─────
Net present value			8,634
			─────

Workings:

Cash flows

Flow $	Probability	$
Year 1		
35,000	0.25	8,750
20,000	0.55	11,000
18,000	0.20	3,600
Expected value		23,350
Year 2		
40,000	0.25	10,000
26,000	0.55	14,300
24,000	0.20	4,800
Expected value		29,100
Year 3		
32,000	0.25	8,000
28,000	0.55	15,400
22,000	0.20	4,400
Expected value		27,800

56   A

Annual cost of capital: 8%

Inflation rate: 3%

Real rate: $(1.08/1.03) - 1 = 0.0485$

Year 1 discount rate:	$1/1.0485$	0.954
Year 2 discount rate:	$1/(1.0485^2)$	0.910
Year 3 discount rate:	$1/(1.0485^3)$	0.868
		2.732

Annual inflow years 1–3: $4,000 \times \$5 = \$20,000$

			Discount rate	$
Year 0	Investment	$50,000	0	50,000
Year 1–3	Inflow	$20,000	2.732	54,640
	NPV			4,640 i.e. $4,500

Alternatively, you can reach the same solution (with some differences possibly for rounding error) by inflating all the cash flows at 3% to their 'out-turn' amount, and discounting these inflated cash flows at the money cost of capital, 8%. The cash flows would be (20,000 × 1.03) $20,600 in year 1, $21,218 in year 2 and $21,855 in year 3.

57 $60,000

Year	Cash ($000)	17% discount factor	Present value ($000)
0	(400)	1.000	(400)
1	210	0.855	179.55
2	240	0.731	175.44
3	320	0.624	199.68
			————
			154.67

Maximum PV of advertising expenditure = $154,670.

Annualise by dividing by annuity factor for years 0 to 2 = 1 + 0.855 + 0.731 = 2.586.

Therefore, maximum cash = $154,670 ÷ 2.586 = $59,811, or $60,000 (rounded to the nearest $000).

58 $8,503

NPV = $0

Let $x be annual rent. The annuity factor for year 5 at 17% is 3.199.

∴ $x × 3.199 = 27,200

∴ $x = 8,503

59 8.9%

Contribution per annum	=	$320,000 + $160,000
	=	$480,000
Contribution per unit	=	$180 − $60
	=	$120 per unit
∴ Level of activity	=	$\dfrac{\$480,000}{\$120}$ = 4,000 units

NPV can fall by $244,170.

Converted to annual cash equivalent:

$$= \frac{\$244,170}{3.791} = \$64,408 \text{ per annum}$$

∴ Unit selling price can fall by up to:

$$\frac{\$64,408}{4,000 \text{ units}} = \$16.10 \text{ per unit}$$

As a percentage: $\dfrac{\$16.10}{\$180} \times 100$ = 8.9%

60 The company's real cost of capital is

$$2.88 \;\%$$

The net present value of the project, when discounting money cash flow at the money rate:

$$\$ \quad 15,473$$

The net present value of the project, when discounting real cash flow at the real rate:

$$\$ \quad 15,387$$

Workings:

$$(1 + \text{real rate}) = \frac{(1+\text{money rate})}{(1+\text{inflation rate})}$$

$$= \frac{1.07}{1.04}$$

$$= 1.0288$$

∴ Real rate = 2.88% per annum.

Discounting money cash flow at the money rate:

Money cash flow		Discount factor at 7%	Present value
Yr 0	(500,000)	1	(500,000)
Yr 1	$130,000 \times 1.04 = 135,200$	0.935	126,412
Yr 2	$130,000 \times 1.04^2 = 140,608$	0.873	122,751
Yr 3	$130,000 \times 1.04^3 = 146,232$	0.816	119,325
Yr 4	$130,000 \times 1.04^4 = 152,082$	0.763	116,039
	Net present value		(15,473)

Alternatively, discounting real cash flow at the real rate

		Discount factor 2.88%	Present value
Yr 0	(500,000)	1	(500,000)
Yr 1–4	130,000	3.7278 (W1)	484,612
	Net present value		(15,387)

Annuity factor for a discount rate of 2.88% for four years is calculated using the formula $(1 - (1 + 0.0288)^{-4})/0.0288$

61 A

This question requires the relationship between money rates and real rates:

1 + r = 1 + i/1 + h where: r = real rate, i = money rate, h = inflation rate.

Rearranged, this gives   1+ h = 1 + i/1 + r

1+ h = 1 + 0.12/1 + 0.06 so h = 5.66%

62 The answer is $17,622.

Capital allowance in Year 2:

Year	Written down value	Capital allowance	Tax saving	Cash timing
1	$75,000	$25,000	$7,500	$3,750
2	$56,250	$18,750	$5,625	$3,750 + $2,812.50
				$2,812.50

Year	Capital allowance benefit	Annual cash inflow	Corporation tax	Net cash	Discount factor	Present value
2	$6,562.50	$20,000	$(6,000)	$20,562.50	0.857	$17,622

63 **C**

Profitability index = NPV per $ invested = $140,500/$500,000 = 0.28

64 $13,112

1.11/1.X6	=	1.0472
Real rate	=	4.72%

$$\frac{1-(1+r)^{-n}}{r}$$

Annuity factor	=	$\dfrac{1-(1.0472)^{-10}}{0.0472}$
	=	7.8278

NPV = $40,000 × 7.8278 − $300,000 = $13,112

65 The internal rate of return of the project is $10\% + \dfrac{\$12,304}{(\$12,304+\$3,216)}\times(15-10)\% = 14\%$

66 The IRR is approximately 26%

NPV at 10% = $87,980

Discounting the cash flows using a higher discount rate, say 20% gives:

Year	Cash flow $	DF	PV $
0	(200,000)	1.000	(200,000)
1	80,000	0.833	66,640
2	90,000	0.694	62,460
3	100,000	0.579	57,900
4	60,000	0.482	28,920
5	40,000	0.402	16,080
			32,000

Using the formula:

$$IRR \approx A + (B - A)\frac{N_A}{N_A - N_B}$$

Where A = lower discount rate (10%)

B = higher discount rate (20%)

N_A = NPV at rate A (87,980)

N_B = NPV at rate B (32,000)

IRR (%) = 20 + (10 × 87,980/55,980) = 26%

67 B

Profits in Year 1 = -$2,000 – depreciation ($60,000/10) = –$8,000

Profits in Year 2 = $13,000 – depreciation $6,000 = $7,000

Profits in Year 3 = $20,000 – depreciation $6,000 = $14,000

Profits in Years 4 to 6 = $25,000 – depreciation $6,000 = $19,000

Profits in Years 7 to 10 = $30,000 – depreciation $6,000 = $24,000

Average profits = (–$8,000 + $7,000 + $14,000 + ($19,000 × 3) + (24,000 × 4))/10

Average profits = $16,600

The investment in Year 1 is $60,000 and the investment in Year 10 is nil. The average investment is therefore $60,000/2 = $30,000. The ARR is therefore $16,600/$30,000 = 55%

68 D

ARR will vary with specific accounting policies, and the extent to which project costs are capitalised. Profit measurement is thus 'subjective', and ARR figures for identical projects could vary from business to business depending on the accounting policies used.

ARR does not provide a definite investment signal. The decision to invest or not is subjective since there is no objectively set target ARR, only a target ARR based on the preferences of management.

ARR fails to take account of either the project life or the timing of cash flows (and time value of money) within that life. For example, a project with a very long life which has a high ARR might be accepted before a project with a shorter life and marginally lower ARR. The NPV of the shorter project may actually be higher.

ARR does have a relationship with other measures used to assess business success. Return on capital employed, which is calculated annually to assess a business or sector of a business (and therefore the investment decisions made by that business), is widely used and its use for investment appraisal is consistent with that.

69 D

Statement 1 is false; ARR places equal value on all cash flows throughout a project's life. NPV places less value on later cash flows. Statement 2 is true: the IRR is the rate that equates the present value of inflows with the present value of the initial outflows. If the IRR is greater than the cost of capital, later cash flows would have been discounted too much.

70 Payback period for Project A: 3 years 4 months

Discounted payback for Project B: 4.47 years

IRR = 15%

Workings:

Year	$000	$000
0	(400)	(400)
1	100	(300)
2	120	(180)
3	140	(40)
4	120	80

Payback period = 3 years + 40/120ths of year 4 = **3.33 years or 3 years 4 months**

Discounted cash flows are:

Year	$000	Present value $000	Cumulative present value $000
0	(450 × 1)	(450)	(450)
1	130 × 0.909	118.17	(331.83)
2	130 × 0.826	107.38	(224.45)
3	130 × 0.751	97.63	(126.82)
4	130 × 0.683	88.79	(38.03)
5	130 × 0.621	80.73	42.70

Discounted payback occurs in year 5 and can be estimated as:

4 years plus 38.03/80.73 of year five = 4.47 years

NPV at 10% is given as $48,000 in the question. Since the NPV is positive the IRR must be higher. If we try discounting at 20%:

Year	Cash flow $000	Discount factor	Present value $000
0	(350)	1.000	(350)
1	50	0.833	42
2	110	0.694	76
3	130	0.579	75
4	150	0.482	72
5	100	0.402	40
NPV			(45)

IRR = 10% + [48/(48 + 45) × (20 − 10)%] = **15% (approx)**

71   C

Investment	J	K	L	M	N
	$000	$000	$000	$000	$000
Initial investment	400	350	450	500	600
Net present value (NPV)	125	105	140	160	190
Profitability index (NPV per $ invested)	0.3125	0.30	0.3111	0.32	0.3166
Ranking	3	4		1	2

J would be chosen before L and, as they are mutually exclusive, L can be disregarded.

The optimum investment plan is $500,000 in M and the remaining $500,000 in N.

72   B

Project	EV	Workings
	$000	
L	500	(500 × 0.2) + (470 × 0.5) + (550 × 0.3)
M	526	(400 × 0.2) + (550 × 0.5) + (570 × 0.3)
N	432.5	(450 × 0.2) + (400 × 0.5) + (475 × 0.3)
O	398	
P	497.5	

Project M will maximise expected cash.

73   1.5 years payback period

Tutorial note

One of the advantages of the payback technique is that it uses cash flows, not subjective accounting profits. You must remember to add the non-cash depreciation to your annual profits when calculating your yearly cash flows.

Depreciation is not a cash flow so needs to be added back to profit to calculate cash flows.

Depreciation on straight line basis = ($400,000 − $50,000)/5 = $70,000 per year

Year	Profit ($)	Cash flow ($)	Cumulative cash flow ($)
0		(400,000)	(400,000)
1	175,000	245,000	(155,000)
2	225,000	295,000	140,000

Payback period = 1 + 155/295 years = 1.5 years to nearest 0.1 years

74   B

75   The present value of a $1 perpetuity is 1/r; The present value of the rental income is $80,000/0.08 = $1,000,000. Therefore, the NPV of the investment is $1,000,000 − $850,000 = $150,000.

76 HURON

A

The projects selected should be the combination of projects with the greatest total NPV, subject to the constraint that the total initial outlay must not exceed $570,000. The other constraint is that projects A and E are mutually exclusive.

Project combination	Total expected NPV	Total outlay
D, E and F	$18,777	$510,000
A, B and F	$13,225	$576,000
A, D and F	$19,637	$576,000
A, D and E (*)	$20,134	$606,000

(*) This should have been rejected outright, as projects A and E are mutually exclusive.

77 C and E

The replacement analysis model assumes that the firm replaces like with like each time it needs to replace an existing asset. However:

- Rapid technological advances mean that up to date models of machine may have different levels of efficiency (even different functions) which would make comparisons difficult

- High inflation would alter the cost structure of the different assets over time but here inflation is very low

- If firms cannot predict with accuracy the market environment they will be facing in the future and whether they will even need to make use of the asset at that time, longer lasting machines may be chosen and yet turn out to be of no use.

The limited resale market and the increases in repair and maintenance costs can be built into the replacement calculations.

78

One year replacement cycle		
	0	1
Buy asset	$(20,000)	
Running costs		$(5,000)
Trade-in		$16,000
Net cash flow	$(20,000)	$11,000
DF @ 10%	1	0.909
PV	$(20,000)	$9,999
NPV	(10,001)	

The Equivalent Annual Cost can be calculated as $10,001/1 year AF = $10,001/0.909 = $11,002. We may compare this EAC with that of a 2-year replacement cycle below:

Two year replacement cycle			
	0	1	2
Buy asset	$(20,000)		
Running costs		$(5,000)	$(5,500)
Trade-in			$13,000
Net cash flow	$(20,000)	$(5,000)	$7,500
DF @ 10%	1	0.909	0.826
PV	$(20,000)	$(4,545)	6,195
NPV	(18,350)		

The Equivalent Annual Cost can be calculated as $18,350/2 year AF = $18,350/1.736 = $10,570.

This EAC is lower than the 1-year replacement cycle EAC. Therefore, the machine should be replaced after 2 years.

79   The optimal replacement period is every two years.

One year replacement cycle		
	0	1
Buy asset	$(12,000)	
Maintenance costs		$0
Trade-in		$9,000
Net cash flow	$(12,000)	$9,000
DF @ 15%	1	0.870
PV	$(12,000)	$7,830
NPV	$ (4,170)	

The Equivalent Annual Cost can be calculated as $4,170/1 year AF = $10,001/0.870 = $4,793. We may compare this EAC with that of a 2-year replacement cycle below:

Two year replacement cycle			
	0	1	2
Buy asset	$(12,000)		
Maintenance costs		$(1,500)	
Trade-in			$7,500
Net cash flow	$(12,000)	$(1,500)	$7,500
DF @ 15%	1	0.870	0.756
PV	$(12,000)	$(1,305)	5,670
NPV	(7,635)		

The Equivalent Annual Cost can be calculated as $7,635/2 year AF = $7,635/1.626 = $4,696. We may compare this EAC with that of a 3-year replacement cycle below:

Two year replacement cycle				
	0	1	2	3
Buy asset	$(12,000)			
Maintenance costs		$(1,500)	$(2,700)	
Trade-in				$7,000
Net cash flow	$(12,000)	$(1,500)	$(2,700)	$7,000
DF @ 15%	1	0.870	0.756	0.658
PV	$(12,000)	$(1,305)	$(2,041)	$4,606
NPV	$(10,740)			

The Equivalent Annual Cost can be calculated as $10,740/3 year AF = $10,740/2.283 = $4,704.

80   D

Equivalent annual cost = (Present value of all costs)/Annuity factor for year 8.

The annuity factor for year 8 (denominator) can be read from the present value and cumulative present value tables, in the 20% column: 3.837 cash flows can be listed as follows:

Initial cost of the machine $150,000, PV $150,000.

Machine resale value $30,000 after 8 years, PV = $30,000 × DF 8@20% so PV = $30,000 × 0.233 = $6,990

Annual running costs $6,000 for the first three years of use: their PV can be calculated as $6,000 × CDF 3 years @ 20% so PV = $6,000 × 2.106 = $12,636

Annual running costs $8,000 for each of the next five years: their PV can be calculated as $8,000 × (CDF 8 years @ 20% − CDF 3 years @ 20%) so PV = $8,000 × (3.837 − 2.106) = $13,848

Therefore, Equivalent annual cost = (−$150,000 + $6,990 − $12,636 − $13,848)/AF 3.837

EAC = $44,173, or $44,200 to the nearest $100.

81   B

Companies considering the replacement of an asset may be faced with alternatives where the life spans of the various machines differ, but the asset is required for the foreseeable future. The options must be evaluated over a comparable number of years.

In order to compare like with like, an equivalent annual cost is calculated as:

PV of costs/Annuity factor for the number of years of use.

This is similar to an average annual cash flow. Once the machines' costs have been annualised the cheapest machine will be the one with the lowest annual cost.

82   A

Depreciation must be added back to the annual profit figures to derive the annual cash flows. Annual depreciation = $(110,400 – 9,600)/4 years = $25,200

Adding $25,200 to each year's profit figure produces the following cash flows:

	Cash flow	Cumulative cash flows
	$	$
Initial investment	(110,400)	(110,400)
Year 1	64,800	(45,600)
Year 2	44,800	(800)
Year 3	47,600	43,800

Payback period   = 2 years + (800/47,600) = 2.01 years

Tutorial note

If you selected a payback period of 3.89 years you based your calculations on the accounting profits after the deduction of depreciation. The calculation of the payback period should be based on cash flows.

Accounting rate of return (ARR)

Average profit	= $(39,600 + 19,600 + 22,400 + 32,400)/4	= $28,500
Average investment	= $(110,400 + 9,600)/2	= $60,000
ARR	= $(28,500/60,000) × 100%	= 47.5%

Tutorial note

If you selected an ARR of 25.8% you calculated the ARR using the opening investment rather than the average investment.

83   D

Net Present Value

Year	Cash flow $	Discount factor 15%	Present value $
0	(12,000)	1.000	(12,000)
1	(4,800)	0.870	(4,176)
2	16,800	0.756	12,701
3	14,400	0.658	9,475
Net Present Value (NPV)			6,000

Tutorial note

If you selected an NPV of $4,440 you treated the $12,000 cash flow as occurring in year 1 and discounted it. Cash flows occurring 'now' should not be discounted.

Year	Present value (PV) $	Cumulative PV $
0	(12,000)	(12,000)
1	(4,176)	(16,176)
2	12,701	(3,475)
3	9,475	6,000

DPP   = 2 years + ((3,475/9,475) × 1 year)
             = 2.36 years

Tutorial note

If you selected 2.0 years you calculated the non-discounted payback period.

84   D

For a standard project, where the IRR is greater than the company's cost of capital, the project will have a positive NPV which means it will increase (rather than maintain) shareholders' wealth (this is not the same thing as earning a profit – profit is an accounting term and does not reflect the impact on cash flows). The IRR indicates the actual return earned by a project and if it is higher than the company's target rate (cost of capital) then it is worth undertaking. IRR gives no indication of speed of payback.

85   A

If money is invested in an account, it will earn interest. However, inflation will have the effect of reducing the value of the return. By deflating the future cash (money) we can find the real return required from the investment, i.e. the required return at today's prices.

86   A

The calculation finds the IRR where a cash outflow is followed by annual cash inflows in perpetuity using the following equation:

The present value of an investment = (Annual cash inflow/discount rate) – Initial investment

Where the discount rate is the IRR, the present value of the investment is zero, leading to the following: 0 = (Annual cash inflow/IRR) – Initial investment

Initial investment = Annual cash inflow/IRR

IRR = Annual cash inflow/Initial investment

87   C

IRR is based on discounted cash flow principles. It therefore considers all of the cash flows in a project (A), does not include notional accounting costs such as depreciation (B) and it considers the time value of money (D). It is not an absolute measure of return, however, as IRR is expressed as a percentage. Two projects can have the same IRR, but very different cash flows.

88   A and C

MIRR measures the economic yield of an investment under the assumption that any cash surpluses are reinvested at the firm's current cost of capital.

MIRR, like IRR, cannot replace net present value as the principle evaluation technique although it does give a measure of the maximum cost of finance that the firm could sustain and allow the project to remain worthwhile.

It does offer some advantages over the standard IRR. Unlike IRR, there will only be one unique MIRR and it does give a measure of the return from a project.

However, the decision criterion requires knowledge of the company's cost of capital as projects should be accepted only when the MIRR (project return) exceeds the company's cost of capital. MIRR does not provide a measure of liquidity and risk, that is one of the advantages of using payback.

89   The first statement is not true and describes the IRR, not the MIRR; The MIRR measures the economic yield of an investment under the assumption that any cash surpluses are reinvested at the firm's current cost of capital.

90   ONTARIO

D

Tutorial note

There are several ways of calculating the MIRR, but CIMA recommends students use the following formula:

MIRR = [(Terminal value of inflows/Present Value of outflows) $^{1/n}$] – 1

	T_0	T_1	T_2	T_3	T_4	**Total**
	($22,500)	$7,500	$7,500	$7,400	$7,300	
Inflow/ Outflow?	Outflow	Inflow	Inflow	Inflow	Inflow	
Terminal value of inflow	–	$7,500 × $(1 + 7\%)^3$ = $9,187.82	$7,500 × $(1 + 7\%)^2$ = $8,586.75	$7,400 × $(1 + 7\%)$ = $7,918	$7,300	$32,992.57
DF @ 7%	1	0.935	0.873	0.816	0.763	
PV of cash flows	($22,500)	$7,012.5	$6,547.5	$6,038.4	$5,569.9	

Terminal value of inflows (from T1 to T4) = $32,992.57

Present value of outflow (at T0) = $22,500

MIRR = [(Terminal value of inflows/Present Value of outflows) $^{1/n}$] – 1

MIRR = [($32,992.57/$22,500)$^{1/4}$] – 1

MIRR = 10.04%

Tutorial note

An alternative calculation, based on a different formula, reads as follows:

Present Value of cash flows from Year 1 to Year 4, or 'PVR' = $25,168.30

Present Value of the 'Investment Phase' of the project, or 'PVI' = $22,500

MIRR = [[PVR/PVI]$^{1/n}$ × (1+re)] –1, where re = the firm's cost of capital, so 7% in our case.

Here, MIRR = [[$25,168.30/$22,500]$^{1/4}$ × (1+7\%)] – 1

MIRR = 10.04%

91   A

Tutorial note

There are several ways of calculating the MIRR, but CIMA recommends students use the following formula:

$MIRR = [(Terminal\ value\ of\ inflows/Present\ Value\ of\ outflows)^{1/n}] - 1$

	T_0	T_1	T_2	T_3	T_4	**Total**
	($67,000)	$20,000	$19,500	$19,000	$19,000	
Inflow/ Outflow?	Outflow	Inflow	Inflow	Inflow	Inflow	
Terminal value of inflows	–	$20,000 × $(1 + 9\%)^3$ = $25,900.58	$19,500 × $(1 + 9\%)^2$ = $23,167.95	$19,000 × $(1 + 9\%)$ = $20,710	$19,000	$88,778.53
DF @ 9%	1	0.917	0.842	0.772	0.708	
PV of cash flows	($67,000)	$18,340	$16,419	$14,668	$13,452	

Terminal value of inflows (from T1 to T4) = $88,778.53

Present value of outflow (at T0) = $67,000

$MIRR = [(Terminal\ value\ of\ inflows/Present\ Value\ of\ outflows)^{1/n}] - 1$

$MIRR = [(\$88,778.53/\$67,000)^{1/4}] - 1$

$MIRR = 7.29\%$

Tutorial note

An alternative calculation, based on a different formula, reads as follows:

Present Value of cash flows from Year 1 to Year 4, or 'PVR' = $62,879

Present Value of the 'Investment Phase' of the project, or 'PVI' = $67,000

MIRR = $[[PVR/PVI]^{1/n} × (1+re)] -1$, where re = the firm's cost of capital, so 9% in our case.

Here, MIRR = $[[\$62,879/\$67,000]^{1/4} × (1+9\%)] -1$

MIRR = 7.29%

92   A

Tutorial note

There are several ways of calculating the MIRR, but CIMA recommends students use the following formula:

MIRR = [(Terminal value of inflows/Present Value of outflows)$^{1/n}$] – 1

	T_0	T_1	T_2	T_3	T_4	
	($120,000)	$45,000	$35,000	$35,000	$30,000	
Inflow/ Outflow?	Outflow	Inflow	Inflow	Inflow	Inflow	
Terminal value of inflows	–	$45,000 × $(1 + 6\%)^3$ = $53,595.72	$35,000 × $(1 + 6\%)^2$ = $39,326	$35,000 × $(1 + 6\%)$ = $37,100	$30,000	$160,021.72
DF @ 6%	1	0.943	0.890	0.840	0.792	
PV of cash flows	($120,000)	$42,435	$31,150	$29,400	$23,760	

Terminal value of inflows (from T1 to T4) = $160,021.72

Present value of outflow (at T0) = $120,000

MIRR = [(Terminal value of inflows/Present Value of outflows)$^{1/n}$] – 1

MIRR = [($160,021.72/$120,000)$^{1/4}$] – 1

MIRR = 7.46%

Tutorial note

An alternative calculation, based on a different formula, reads as follows:

Present Value of cash flows from Year 1 to Year 4, or 'PVR' = $126,745

Present Value of the 'Investment Phase' of the project, or 'PVI' = $120,000

MIRR = [[PVR/PVI]$^{1/n}$ × (1+re)] –1, where re = the firm's cost of capital, so 6% in our case.

Here, MIRR = [[$126,745/$120,000]$^{1/4}$ × (1+6%)] –1

MIRR = 7.46%

93   A

94   D

The company uses NPV to evaluate its projects and thus the fact that Project B has a higher IRR is not relevant. Additionally, one of the assumptions underlying NPV is that sufficient funds are available to undertake all profitable investments – the company can therefore appraise both projects on their own merits and does not need to reject Project A just because it is expected to perform less well than Project B. It is true that Project A will not increase shareholder wealth – but it will earn their required return of 10% and it should therefore be accepted.

95 $5,193.75

	$
Salary costs:	
Senior consultant 75 hours × $45	3,375.00
Junior consultant 30 hours × $26	780.00
Marginal cost	4,155.00
Mark-up (25%)	1,038.75
Price to charge client	5,193.75

96   The cost of making other related products is the only option which would NOT apply.

97   B, D and E

A   If demand is very elastic, high market share and a market presence could be achieved quickly by charging a low-penetration pricing.

B   Here market skimming would be more appropriate. A high price could be charged to the 'opinion leaders' who want to be seen to have the new product and are prepared to pay a high price.

C   It is difficult to charge a low price for a product where there are few opportunities for economies of scale since cost per unit will still be high irrespective of production volume.

D   If demand is inelastic, charging a low price will not have a beneficial effect upon sales volume and profit.

E   If there is little competition and high barriers to entry, such as in the pharmaceutical industry, there is no incentive for companies to charge a low price.

98   B

At first inspection all four appear to be methods of arriving at selling price.

However, target costing is a method to arrive at the cost at which a product should be produced for having worked backwards from the price already set for the product.

It is a method to arrive at product cost not product selling price.

99   A

100 MALTOV

$70

To maximise profit Maltov must produce where MC = MR (MC is Marginal Cost, MR is Marginal Revenue)

MC = $20   MR = $120 – Q

So to maximise profit, $20 = $120 – Q

Therefore, Q = $100.

To calculate the price that must be sold, Price = $120 – 0.5 × quantity

So, Price = $120 – 0.5 × $100 = $120 – $50 = $70

101 C

$40,000

If components are purchased outside:

Contribution earned elsewhere	$25,000
Variable cost saving	$15,000
Maximum price to pay	$40,000

102 C

The trust is discriminating on the grounds of market segment (segmenting using occupation).

103

Marginal cost (MC) = $14

Price (P) = $35 – 0.01q

Marginal Revenue (MR) = $35 – 0.02q

So if MC = MR then:

14 = 35 – 0.02q

0.02q = 21

Q = 1,050

Price = $35 – (0.01 × 1,050)   **= $24.50**

104 $300

To solve this, we have to derive an equation as follows:

P = price and let X = demand in units

Then

50p = 50,000 – X

$$p = \frac{50,000 - X}{50}$$

p = 1,000 – 0.02X

We are told that the profit maximising level of sales is 35,000 units, so this is X.

Therefore,

p = 1,000 – 0.02 × 35,000 = 1,000 – 700 = $300

105 SAMSINGING LTD

The price to set which will maximise profit for 'Samsinging Ltd.' can be found by using a table to calculate the profit resulting for the given price and related sales volumes.

Table for sales levels **per month**

Sales quantity

(000 units)	50	100	150	200	250	300	350	400
Price per unit ($)	400	375	350	325	300	275	250	225
Revenue ($m)	20	37.5	52.5	65	75	82.5	87.5	90
Variable production cost per unit ($)	240	240	240	240	240	210	210	210
Variable production costs ($m)	12	24	36	48	60	63	73.5	84
Fixed production costs ($m)	4	4	4	4	4	4.5	4.5	4.5
Variable selling cost per unit ($)	35	35	35	40	40	40	40	40
Variable selling costs ($m)	1.75	3.5	5.25	8	10	12	14	16
Profit ($m)	2.25	6.0	7.25	5.0	1.0	3.0	(4.5)	(14.5)

The maximum profit is $7.25 million if 150,000 units are sold at a price of $350 per unit.

So the company should set a selling price of $350 per unit.

106 STALY PLC

Brompton price: Given that the price and volume of sales has been presented as a table, it makes sense to calculate the profit for each piece and quantity combination also using a tabular approach and then select the price at which the level of profit is maximised.

Brompton Ltd wishes to determine the price at which the new toy should be sold in order to maximise profit. A tabular approach can be used as follows:

Price ($)	5	10	15	20	25	30	35	40
Quantity of units (000)	200	180	160	135	120	100	75	50
Sales $000	1,000	1,800	2,400	2,700	3,000	3,000	2,625	2,000
Variable costs ($6 × no. of units) $000	1,200	1,080	960	810	720	600	450	300
Fixed costs $000	450	450	450	400	400	400	400	400
Profit/(Loss)	(650)	270	990	1,490	1,880	2,000	1,775	1,300

Profit is maximised when the price is set at $30 per unit. This is therefore the price that should be set by Brompton Ltd.

In order for Electrics Ltd to **maximise profit** it should produce where MC = MR

Since Marginal Cost is the addition to cost of making one more unit, this will be the total variable cost of $600 per unit.

MR is given as MR = 2,000 – 0.02Q, So setting MC = MR gives 600 = 2,000 – 0.02Q

2,000 – 600 = 0.02Q

1,400 = 0.02Q

1,400/0.02 = Q

Therefore, Q = 70,000 units

So in order to maximise profit, Electrics Ltd should produce and sell 70,000 units per annum. The selling price should be:

P = 2,000 – 0.01Q

P = 2,000 – 0.01 × 70,000 = 2,000 – 700 = $1,300

So the selling price in order to maximise profit should be $1,300 per computer.

In order for Electrics Ltd to maximise revenue it should produce where MR = 0

That is, 2,000 – 0.02Q = 0

So 2,000 = 0.02Q

2,000/0.02 = Q

Q = 100,000 units

At a price of P = 2,000 – 0.01Q

P = 2,000 – 0.01 × 100,000

P = 2,000 – 1,000 = $1,000

In order to maximise revenue, Electrics Ltd should produce and sell 100,000 computers at a price of $1,000 per computer.

107 AVX LTD

$1,096.36

The marginal cost and selling price per batch are as follows:

Marginal cost = $672.72

Demand at price of $1,200 = 16 batches and demand increases by 1 unit for every $20 reduction in selling price.

Therefore, Price = $1,520 – 20q   Marginal Revenue = $1,520 – 40q

Equating marginal cost and marginal revenue:

672.72 = 1,520 – 40q   40q = 847.28

q = 21.182   Price = $1,520 – (20 × 21.182) = **$1,096.36**

108 MtF

A

First find X using MC=MR. Marginal Cost is 25 and the Marginal Revenue function is found from MR = a – 2bX or MR = 85 – 0.1X

MC = MR; 25 = 85 – 0.1X Rearrange equation: 0.1X = 85 – 25; 0.1X = 60 so X = 60/0.1 = 600

Revert to demand function P = 85 – (0.05 × 600), so P = 85 – 30 i.e. P = 55

109   C

110   P   Profit maximising price

a   Intercept on the y axis (price where sales = zero)

b   Slope of the demand curve

X   Profit Maximising Quantity

111 $900

First, we must find the elements of the demand curve: b = 30/150 = 0.2

To find 'a' substitute when Price = zero, demand = 15,000 (where the line cuts the x axis). i.e.

0 = a – (0.2 × 15,000)   0 = a – 3,000   a = 3,000   P = 3000 – 0.2X

And when profit is maximised P = 3,000 – (0.2 × 10,500) = 900

112   XYZ MOTOR GROUP

NV (New Vehicle division)

	$	
Margin on new vehicle	8,000	(40,000 × 20%)
Trade in value given	–28,000	
Transfer price	16,675	(17,500 – 825)
Total	**–3,325**	

UV (Used Vehicle division)

	$
Sale proceeds	28,900
Repair costs	–825
Transfer price	–16,675
Total	**11,400**

VR (Vehicle Repair division)

	$
Repairs invoiced	825
Variable costs	–500
Total	**325**

XYZ Motor Group

	$
NV	–3,325
UV	11,400
VR	000325
Total	**8,400**

C: MANAGING AND CONTROLLING THE PERFORMANCE OF ORGANISATIONAL UNITS

113 B

(i), (ii) and (iii) only. Apportioned head office costs are not controllable by the manager of an investment centre. Discretionary fixed costs (those which do not have to be incurred in the short term, such as advertising and training) are within the manager's control, since they can be increased or reduced at fairly short notice.

The level of inventory in the division is a part of the capital invested in the division, which is usually controllable by the manager of an investment centre. The manager also has control over the revenue from sales within the organisation (transfer prices).

114 B

Cost centres have the lowest degree of autonomy with managers only able to control costs. Profit centres have a higher degree of autonomy as managers can not only control costs, but can also control sales prices and revenue. Investment centres have the highest degree of autonomy as managers can not only control costs and revenues but can also make investment decisions not open to managers in either of the other two centres.

115 56%

It would appear that the company should cease producing product YY since it generates a loss. However, for decision-making, contribution should always be used instead of profit.

If the entire $9,000 of fixed cost is avoidable then the company should cease producing N since it will forego contribution of $5,000 but save fixed costs of $9,000 so being $4,000 better off overall.

If, say, only $4,000 of the fixed costs are avoidable, ceasing production of YY would result in loss of contribution of $5,000 but save fixed costs of $4,000 so the company would be $1,000 worse off. Here they should continue production of YY. Since contribution from YY is $5,000 at a minimum the avoidable fixed cost would have to be $5,000.

As a percentage this is $5,000/$9,000 × 100% = 56%.

116 HULME

Division H should be closed and all other divisions should be kept open.

If a division is closed the company will forego any contribution it was expected to generate but it will save any fixed cost that is incurred specifically by that division (no division, no specific fixed cost!).

Therefore, we must look at contribution with less specific fixed costs for each division to see what will be foregone if the division is closed.

	Division T	Division H	Division E
	$000	$000	$000
Contribution	150	120	50
Specific fixed costs			
(80% × 450 = 360, 360/8 × 3, 4, 1)	(135)	(180)	(45)
	15	(60)	5

So, if Division T were to be closed the company will forego $15,000.

If Division E were closed the company will forego $5,000.

Therefore, both of these divisions should be kept open.

However, if Division H is closed the company will forego $120,000 of contribution but save specific fixed costs of $180,000 – a net saving of $60,000.

So, Division H should be closed.

117

The ratio is at its lowest when debtors are low and creditors high. Thus the debtors ($135,000) must be double the combined overdraft and creditors (i.e. $67,500).

O/d = $67,500 – $22,000 = $45,500.

Or using algebra, 135,000 = 2(22,000 + o/d)

67,500 = 22,000 + o/d

o/d = 45,500.

118

You need to know the relationship between these ratios. Return on investment = net profit margin × asset turnover

Thus Net profit margin = return on investment ÷ asset turnover

= 18%/2 = 9%.

119 B

The manager of a profit centre can exercise control over revenues and controllable costs, but has no influence concerning the capital invested in the centre.

Contribution (i) would be a useful performance measure because a profit centre manager can exercise control over sales revenue and variable costs. Controllable profit (ii) would also be useful as long as any overhead costs charged in deriving the profit figure are controllable by the profit centre manager. Apportioned central costs would not be deducted when calculating controllable profit. Return on investment (iii), residual income (iv) and economic value added (v) would not be useful because they require a measure of the capital invested in the division.

120 Remember that the current ratio is current assets/current liabilities.

Here the only liabilities seem to be creditors = $144,000

Current assets must be 1.7 × 144,000 = 244,800

Bank must be 244,800 − 14,800 − 19,600 = 210,400.

121 You need to know the relationship between these ratios.

Return on investment = net profit margin × asset turnover

$$= 16\% \times 0.9$$

$$= 14.4\%.$$

122 Return on investment = Asset turnover × Net profit margin.

Therefore ROI = 5 × 4% = 20%

ROI also = Operating profit/Capital employed

$$0.2 = \frac{£80,000}{x}$$

x = $400,000

123

The operating profit margin for the budget period	**16.5**	%
The total net asset turnover for the period	**2.05**	times
The budgeted current ratio	**2.03**	times
The budgeted quick (acid test) ratio	**0.97**	times

Operating profit margin = 900/5,440 × 100% = 16.5%

	$000	$000
Non-current assets		1,850
Current assets		
Inventory	825	
Receivables	710	
Bank	50	
		1,585
		3,435
Less current liabilities		(780)
		2,655

Net asset turnover = 5,440/2,655 = 2.05 times

Current ratio = 1,585/780 = 2.03 times; Acid test/quick ratio = (1,585 – 825)/780 = 0.97 times

124 DB Holdings Ltd – key business metrics

	2013	2014
ROCE (Operating profit/Capital employed)	6.72	10.00
Operating profit margin (Operating profit/Revenue)	6.67	7.24
Current liquidity ratio (Current assets/Current liabilities)	3.7	2.1*
Receivables days (Receivable/Sales)	24	62
Inventory days (Inventory/Purchases**)	46	73
Payable days (Payables/Purchases**)	23	53
Cash conversion period	47	82

(Inventory days + receivables days – payables days)

*Note that the overdraft in 2014 means that the company liabilities amount to 180 + 780 = 960

**Approximated as Sales – Operating profit

Note:

- In certain cases an approximate figure is used. For example, in calculating inventory days and payables days one needs to know 'purchases' – but since this is unavailable, operating costs are used instead.

  Operating costs = Sales – Operating profit.

  Since most business costs are purchases, the resultant inventory and payables days figures are meaningful and allow a clear inter-period comparison.

- Inventory and payables days positions for 2013 are both based on year-end figures. Ideally we would base these figures on an average of end 2013 and end 2014 balances. However, these figures are not available, and year-end figures are deemed a suitable approximation.

125 The ROI of the investment is $128,000/$855,000 = 15%.

Thus the manager's performance will appear to decline if they take on this project (their new return will fall below the existing 17%). They will therefore reject this investment.

However, a return of 15% is beneficial to the company, and so the manager rejects to the detriment of the company.

126 The ROI of the investment is $15,000/$135,000 = 11%.

Thus the manager's performance will appear to improve if they take on this project (their new return will rise above the existing 8%). They will therefore accept this investment.

However, a return of 11% is detrimental to the company, and so the manager accepts to the detriment of the company.

127 The ROI of the investment is $28,000/$155,000 = 18%.

This will reduce the division's ROI and will cause the manager to reject.

The RI is $28,000 − 15% × $155,000 = $4,750.

Since this is positive the manager will accept.

128 A

It is worth noting that you do not need the figures to work this question out (although you can use them if you want).

(i)   Paying now would reduce creditors and thus increase capital employed, leading to lower rates of return. Note that the 'return' of 5% is nowhere near high enough to make this worth considering.

(ii) Scrapping will reduce the capital employed, leading to higher returns, the income will just accentuate this.

129 Each manager will only consider costs that are variable to them, fixed costs will be ignored – they are unavoidable.

Manager A will want to produce as the transfer price ($12) exceeds their variable cost ($10), adding to their contribution.

Manager B will want to produce as the revenue from the sale ($21) exceeds the variable cost and transfer price ($8 + $12), adding to their contribution.

The company will increase its contribution if production occurs, because the final selling price is greater than the total variable costs.

The position is goal congruent since both divisions wish to produce.

130 B

The internal price is just another name for the TP, so it is not a method of transfer pricing.

131 You must set a price high enough for TM to cover its costs, but not so high that RM cannot make a profit.

For TM, an item sold externally has VC of 60% × $24.00 = $14.40

Of this, $1.50 will not be incurred on an internal transfer so it is not relevant here, VC on internal transfer = $14.40 – $1.50 = $12.90

We do not know RM's cost structure, so we leave the price at $12.90; this will ensure that RM is not discouraged from taking an internal transfer when it is profitable to do so.

132 (i)   A can sell all of its output into the intermediate market at $180, so the TP needs to exceed this.

B needs to make a contribution so the TP needs to be below $290 – $80 = $210

So, $180 to $210 range.

(ii)   A needs to cover its costs, so TP must exceed $150.

B can buy from the intermediate market at $180, so the TP must be lower than this.

So, $150 to $180 range.

133 D

Divisional managers will be more aware of changes in the environment in which their own part of the business operates. Thus a decentralised organisation can respond more rapidly to local environmental changes than can a centralised organisation.

A problem with decentralisation tends to be that managers will give priority to the performance of their own centre, even if an improvement in their own performance can cause a worse performance for the organisation overall. Goal congruence can be difficult to achieve in a decentralised organisation and option A is therefore incorrect.

The selection of non-subjective performance measures can be a problem in a decentralised organisation, therefore option B is incorrect.

Communication can be difficult in a decentralised organisation, especially if the various divisions are geographically widespread. Therefore option C is incorrect.

134 18.7%

Return on investment = profit before interest and tax (PBIT)/capital employed

PBIT = $320,000 + $200,000 + $100,000 + $70,000 = $690,000

Capital employed = $2.69m + $1.00m = $3.69m

ROI = 690,000/3,690,000 × 100% = 18.7%

135 B

Original profit	=	$2,000,000 × 12%	=	$240,000
New profit	=	$240,000 + $90,000	=	$330,000
New capital employed	=	$2,000,000 + $500,000	=	$2,500,000
Residual income	=	$330,000 – (10% × $2,500,000)	=	$80,000

136 C

ROI before project	=	360/1,600	=	22.5%
ROI after project	=	385/(1,600 + 130)	=	22.3%

Therefore management would reject this project, if ROI is used as an evaluation criterion.

Residual value before project	=	360 – (1,600 × 0.18)	=	$72,000
Residual value after project	=	385 – (1,730 × 0.18)	=	$73,600

Therefore management would accept this project if residual income is used as an evaluation criterion.

137 C

$$ROI = \frac{\text{Profit before interest and tax}}{\text{Operations management capital employed}}$$

Profit before interest and tax is the reported profit of the division calculated by 'normal' accounting rules, based only on controllable figures.

The operations management capital employed is the capital employed for which the centre manager is responsible and accountable.

Capital employed can be calculated as equity + long-term debt or non-current assets + current assets – current liabilities.

$$ROI = \frac{400}{1,000 + 700} \quad \text{or} \quad \frac{400}{1,500 + 600 - 400} = 23.5\%$$

138 B

	$000
Profit before interest and tax	400
Imputed interest	
12% × 1,700	204
	196

The imputed interest is the cost of capital × capital employed.

139 Controllable profit would be calculated before a charge is made for allocated central costs, over which the division manager cannot exercise control.

Controllable profit = $(35,000 + 25,000) = $60,000

Controllable ROI without the new machine = $60,000/$420,000 = 14.3%

Controllable ROI with the new machine = $(60,000 + 5,500)/(420,000 + 50,000) = 13.9%

Residual income calculations	**Without machine**	**With machine**
	$	$
Controllable profit	60,000	65,500
Interest charge	42,000	47,000
Residual income	18,000	18,500

140 A

	$
Accounting profit	135,000
Less additional depreciation (41,000 – 22,000)	(19,000)
Add back increase in doubtful debt provision	8,000
NOPAT (ignoring tax)	124,000
Replacement cost of net assets	660,000
Add provision for doubtful debts	12,000
Economic value of capital employed	672,000
Cost of capital	× 14%
Capital charge	94,080
NOPAT	124,000
Capital charge	94,080
EVA	29,920

141 D

	$ million
Operating profit	20.2
Add back launch costs	3.0
Less amortisation of launch costs	(1.0)
	22.2
Replacement cost of assets	84.0
Add increase in capitalised launch costs	2.0
	86.0
Cost of capital	× 11%
Capital charge	9.46

EVA = $(22.2 – 9.46) million = $12.74 million

142

(i) Operating profit margin = operating profit/sales × 100%

$(3,629,156/7,055,016) \times 100 = 51.44\%$

(ii) Capital employed = total assets − current liabilities

$4,582,000 + 4,619,582 + 442,443 - 949,339 - 464,692 = 8,229,994$

Return on capital employed = Operating profit/capital employed × 100%

$(3,629,156/8,229,994) \times 100 = 44.10\%$

(iii) Trade receivable days = trade receivables/turnover × 365

$(442,443/7,055,016) \times 365$ days $= 22.89$ days

(iv) Current/liquidity ratio = current assets/current liabilities

$(4,619,582 + 442,443)/(949,339 + 464,692) = 3.58:1$

143 D

An investment centre has responsibility for sales, costs and net assets.

144 B

	Centre 1		Centre 2	
	$		$	$
External sales (300 × $28)	8,400	(150 × $40)		6,000
Transfer sales (150 × $(20 + 20%))	3,600			–
	12,000			6,000
Transfer costs			3,600	
Own costs (450 × $20)	9,000	(150 × $8)	1,200	
				4,800
Profit	3,000			1,200

145 C

Statement (i) is correct. The buying profit centre will incur the same cost when buying from within and outside the business, and so is likely to be indifferent about the source of supply.

Statement (ii) is correct. When there is spare capacity, a transfer price based on incremental cost rather than market price might encourage the buying profit centre to purchase internally in order to utilise spare capacity. A transfer price based on the full market price will not encourage the utilisation of spare capacity to make a marginal additional profit.

146 The annual reduction in divisional profit for Division A amounts to:

$ 45,000

The annual reduction in profit for Company X amounts to:

$ 32,500

Division A will lose the contribution from internal transfers to Division B.

Contribution forgone   =   2,500 × $(40 – 22)

= **$45,000** reduction in profit

	$ per unit
Cost per unit from external supplier	35
Variable cost of internal manufacture saved	22
Incremental cost of external purchase	13

Reduction in profit of X   = $13 × 2,500 units

=   **$32,500**

147 C

The optimum transfer price is where:

Transfer price   =   marginal cost + opportunity cost

The opportunity cost is the contribution forgone from an external sale of alpha = $16

$(6 + 4 + 2) = $4

The optimum transfer price is therefore:

Marginal cost $10 + opportunity cost $4 = $14 per unit

148 A

Marginal cost will be same as Variable cost, that is $15.

The two-part tariff transfer price per unit is marginal cost $15.

149 C

(a) **Two-part tariff system:** The price **per unit** credited to the supplying Division S would be the marginal cost of $28. The agreed fixed fee should be ignored when calculating the **unit** price.

(b) **Dual price:** The price credited to the supplying Division S would be the market price $40. (The element of profit in this ($12) would be removed so that only $28 (the marginal cost) would be debited to Division T.)

150 D

	$
Market price of product N in Canada	300
Less: Total cost	120
Pre-tax profit	180
Post-tax profit per unit ($1,100,000/11,000 units)	100
Tax (balancing figure)	80

Tax as a percentage of pre-tax profit is $80/$180 × 100 = 44%.

151 D

	Per unit £	Per unit £
Market price in UK		250.0
Less: Transfer price at variable cost: $\dfrac{\$120 \times 0.75}{1.5}$	60.0	
UK marketing and distribution costs	40.0	100.0
		150.0
Less: Tax at 25%		(37.5)
		112.5

11,000 units at £112.50 = £1,237,500 profit after tax.

152 A

A higher transfer price will mean that CMW Ltd is charged more for goods transferred, thus decreasing UK profits and increasing the overseas profit.

Increased royalty payments paid by CMW Ltd will decrease UK profits and increase the overseas profit.

153 (i)   Loss is $1,000,000:

Marginal (variable) cost = 70 + 20 + 10 = $100

External selling price = 150 × 1.3333 = $200

		$000
Sales		
Internal	60,000 × $100	6,000
External	40,000 × $200	8,000
		14,000
Variable cost	100,000 × $100	10,000
Contribution		4,000
Fixed costs		
Production	100,000 × $40	4,000
Administration	100,000 × $10	1,000
Loss		(1,000)

(ii)   Profit is $1,400,000.

The total production cost = $140 (not $150 as this includes selling and administration overhead). This means that sales revenue increases by $40 × 60,000 = $2,400,000 and costs stay the same. Profit is now (1,000,000) + 2,400,000 = $1,400,000.

154   The level of sales that would maximise the profit from this service for the Legal Division is 2,000 hours and its contribution would be $30,000.

The level of sales that would maximise the profit from L&S for the KL Company as a whole is 3,000 hours and the contribution would be $75,000.

We are trying to maximise the profit from the service from the Legal Division's point of view. As far as the Legal Division is concerned its variable costs are $65 ($25 + $40).

Hours sold	Price per hour	Variable cost per hour	Contribution per hour	Total contribution
0	100	65	35	0
1,000	90	65	25	25,000
2,000	80	65	15	30,000
3,000	70	65	5	15,000
4,000	60	65	(5)	(20,000)
5,000	50	65	(15)	(75,000)

The level of sales that would maximise the contribution for the Legal Division is 2,000 hours and its contribution would be $30,000.

We are trying to maximise the profit from the service from the group point of view. As far as the group is concerned the variable cost of the service is $45 ($20 + $25).

Hours sold	Price per hour	Variable cost per hour	Contribution per hour	Total contribution
0	100	45	55	0
1,000	90	45	45	45,000
2,000	80	45	35	70,000
3,000	70	45	25	75,000
4,000	60	45	15	60,000
5,000	50	45	5	25,000

The level of sales that would maximise the contribution for the whole company is 3,000 hours and the contribution would be $75,000.

This answer assumes that the Secretarial Division has spare capacity.

155 A

ROI = Net income/Net assets = 300,000/6,750,000 × 100% = 4.44%

156 D

$300,000 – 13% × $6,750,000 = ($577,000)

157 A

EVA = NOPAT – Economic value of assets × Cost of capital

NOPAT	$m
Operating profit	89.2
Add back development costs	+9.6
Less amortisation of development costs	–3.2
Add back accounting depreciation	+24
Less economic depreciation	–33.6
	86

Economic value of assets	$m
Replacement cost of assets	168
Less economic depreciation	–33.6
Add net increase in development costs	+6.4
Add working capital	+27.2
	168

EVA = 86 – 13% × 168 = $64.16m

158 The post-tax profit for X is $483,000 and the post-tax profit for Y is $669,200.

The variable cost of the component = $600 × 0.6 = $360

Transfer price = $360 × 1.7 = $612

$000	X	Y
Sales: External (W1)	8,000	14,400
Internal (W2)	7,344	
	15,344	14,400
Variable cost (W3)	(7,920)	(12,144)
Fixed production cost (W4)	(5,280)	
Fixed non-production cost	(1,500)	(1,300)
Profit before tax	644	956
Tax	(161)	(286.8)
Profit after tax	483	669.2

Workings

(W1) $800 × 10,000 = $8,000,000

$1,200 × 12,000 = $14,400,000

(W2) 12,000 × $612 = $7,344,000

(W3) $360 × 22,000 = $7,920,000

Variable cost for product W = $400 + $612 = $1,012 per unit

$1,012 × 12,000 = $12,144,000

(W4) $240 × 22,000 = $5,280,000

159 The two correct statements are Option 2 'It is commonly used and understood' and option 6 'It can be used to compare projects of different sizes'.

Option 1 is not correct – it is a percentage not an absolute value. Option 3 is not correct – profits are subjective not objective, depending on the accounting policies used. Option 4 is not correct – it is not linked to the overall company cost of capital, so can give non goal congruent decisions and option 5 is not correct– it uses profits, which can be manipulated to change the ROI.

160 The answer is 10.25%. We need to add back the non-controllable head office depreciation and the non-controllable financing costs but not the controllable depreciation on X's assets to get the profit figure.

161 Only statement (iv) is correct.

Statement (i) is not correct: projects with a positive NPV should always be accepted (ignoring risk); Statement (ii) is not correct ; profit centres will not be in control of their investment of capital so shouldn't be evaluated on its use; Statement (iii) is not correct: Tax is not controllable so shouldn't be included in the calculation of ROI.

162 D

Project ROI: Average annual profits = revenue − variable costs − depreciation

Revenue = $20,000 × 12 = $240,000

Variable costs = $5,000 × 12 = $60,000

Depreciation = ($600,000 − $100,000)/5 = $100,000

Annual profit = $240,000 − $60,000 − $100,000 = $80,000

Initial investment less 1 year's depreciation = $600,000 − $100,000 = $500,000

ROI = $80,000/$500,000 × 100 = 16%

Dilutes the existing ROI so would not be accepted.

ROI is not related to cost of capital for evaluation. Plus the cost of capital isn't given, so we couldn't evaluate on that basis.

Evaluating the ROI without the depreciation figure (i.e. using cash flows instead of profits) would give an answer of 36% (or 30% if depreciation isn't deducted from capital to get NBV) which is incorrect as we need to use profits, not cash flows.

163 27%

Profits = annual cash flows − depreciation

Here, depreciation = ($50,000 − $5,000)/5 years = $9,000 per annum.

Annual profits = $20,000 − $9,000 = $11,000

Capital Employed at the end of year 1 = $50,000 − $9,000 = $41,000

ROI = Annual profits/Capital employed

ROI = ($11,000/$41,000) × 100%

ROI = 27%

Tutorial note

Note that we assume that the 'Capital Employed' at the start of the year (i.e. before depreciation is deducted) is the one that was used to generate the profits at the end of the year. Therefore, the opening capital employed is generally used in OT calculations, unless the question directs you otherwise.

164 Options 'A' and 'D' are correct. Profits are subjective rather than objective (as they depend on the accounting policies used) and can be manipulated. As an absolute measure, Residual Income can't be used to compare different sized investments.

165 B

Current profit can be calculated as 0.2 × $1.2 m = $240,000

Current profit + Project A (highest ROI > 20%): ROI = (240 + 100)/(1,200 + 300) = 22.66%

Current profit + Projects A and B (ROI > 22.66%):

ROI = (240 + 100 + 210)/(1,200 + 300 + 700) = 25%

Current profit + Projects A, B and C (ROI > 25%):

ROI = (240 + 100 + 210 + 130)/(1,200 + 300 + 700 + 500) = 25.2%, so we shouldn't add D as ROI < 25.2%

166 C

167 B

Net monthly cash = $7,500 – $4,900 = $2,600

Net annual cash flow = $2,600 × 12 months = $31,200

Annual depreciation = ($100,000 – $10,000)/5 years = $18,000

Annual profit = $31,200 – $18,000 = $13,200

Notional interest charge = $100,000 × 12% = $12,000

Residual income = $13,200 – $12,000 = $1,200

RI is positive so accept.

Bonus is based on RI so irrelevant whether project makes profit or not. ROI is irrelevant.

168 Statements (i) and (iv) apply.

Statements (ii) and (iii) do not apply: ROI does not relate profitability to the cost of capital, and RI is an absolute measure so is distorted by divisional size.

169 The answer is $250,000.

Controllable profits amount to $650,000. Admin recharge and depreciation are not controllable, so we must exclude them. Controllable capital employed $2,000,000; the allocated floor in head office is not a controllable asset, so is excluded.

Controllable RI = $650,000 – ($2,000,000 × 0.2) = $250,000.

170 C

Project A

incremental contribution $20,000

incremental depreciation $12,500

incremental profit $7,500

project RI = $7,500 – $50,000 × 13% = $1,000. RI is positive so accept.

Project B

incremental contribution $200,000

incremental depreciation $30,000

incremental profit $170,000

project RI = $170,000 – $1,500,000 × 13% = $–25,000. RI is negative so reject.

171 B

172 The balanced scorecard approach is a way of providing information to management which involves the inclusion of <u>non-financial</u> information alongside financial information.

It emphasises the need to provide the user with a set of information which addresses <u>all</u> relevant areas of performance in an objective and unbiased fashion.

Although the specific measures used may vary, a scorecard would normally include the following measures

- <u>profitability</u> – the financial perspective

- <u>customer satisfaction</u> – the customer perspective

- innovation – the <u>innovation and learning</u> perspective

- internal efficiency – the <u>internal business</u> perspective.

By providing all this information in a single report, management is able to assess the impact of particular actions on all perspectives of the company's activities. Under each perspective, a company should state its aims and specify measures of performance.

For example:

		Aims	**Measure**
1	Financial perspective	<u>Survival</u>	Current ratio
2	Customer perspective	Satisfaction	<u>Returning customers</u>
3	Internal business perspective	<u>Efficiency</u>	Throughput rates
4	Innovation and learning	New products	<u>Income from new products</u>

173 C

174 Statement (ii) only is true: the RI will increase, because the additional imputed interest charge will be lower than the additional profit generated.

Statement (i) is false, as the ROI and Residual Income might be used as one of the measures within the financial perspective. Statement (iii) is also false, as the internal business perspective monitors what the business must be good at in order to succeed, for example, the average setup time or the speed with which interdepartmental queries are handled. Statement (iv) is false as a disadvantage of residual income is that it does not facilitate comparisons between investment centres. The same absolute value of RI might be earned by two investment centres but it is much easier for a larger investment centre to generate a given level of RI than it is for a smaller investment centre.

175 C

For every unit of Product B not sold internally, Division A would sell an equally profitable Product A externally, so there would be no change in the profits of Division A. The company as a whole would gain ($176 – $140) = $36 per unit on every unit of product A and pay ($152 – $140) = $12 per unit more on every unit of Product B, so gains overall.

176 U PLC

B

To get a constant ROI, both profits and capital should be constant. Reducing balance depreciation would increase profits over the life. Net book value would decrease the capital figure.

177 MCG PLC

All statements are true and apply to MCG plc.

178 C

Value for money relates to economy (value for money on inputs to the organisation), efficiency (vfm on converting inputs to outputs) and effectiveness (vfm on the outputs). Economy relates to keeping costs down without sacrificing quality, efficiency is about effective resource utilisation (such as decreasing waste levels) and effectiveness relates to the overall objectives of the organisation being achieved.

D: RISK AND CONTROL

179

Statements	True	False
Only risk seekers will invest in risky projects.		✓
If an investment has a 60% chance of earning $100 and a 40% chance of losing $20, a risk neutral investor would be willing to pay $52 to make that investment.	✓	
If an investment has a 60% chance of earning $100 and a 40% chance of losing $20, a risk averse investor would be willing to pay $52 to make that investment.		✓

180 B

Inventing a simple project which fulfils the criteria, for example t0 (1,000), t1 1,100; and revising the t1 cash flow to include 9% inflation rather than 4%, the project becomes:

t0 (1,000), t1 1,153 being (1,100/1.04) × 1.09.

The new internal rate of return is 15.3%.

Tutorial note

Alternatively, you could say the IRR of 10% is a money rate, so our 'real' IRR is 1.10/1.04 − 1 = 5.8%. if inflation changes to 9% then our new money IRR is 1.058 × 1.09 − 1 = 15.3%..

181 D

Year	Cash	15%	PV
	$		$
0	(75,000)		(75,000)
1 − 5	25,000	3.352	83,800
			8,800

Try 20%

Year	Cash	20%	PV
	$		$
0	(75,000)		(75,000)
1 − 5	25,000	2.991	74,775
			(225)

182 C

$$IRR = 15\% + \frac{8,800}{(8,800+225)} \times 5\%$$

$$IRR = 15\% + \frac{8,800}{9,025} \times 5\%$$

IRR = 19.88%

PV of labour cost = $20,000 × 3.352

= $67,040

∴ Allowable change $= \frac{8,800}{67,040} \times 100 \quad = \textbf{13.13\%}$

183 A

Sensitivity = NPV/**present value** of the flow under consideration. Therefore, we need the PV of labour costs of $20,000 p.a. for five years, and we can use annuity factor.

$20,000 × 3.791 = $75,820   Sensitivity therefore is 8,800/75,820 = **11.61%**.

184 7.93%

If the present value of the labour costs falls by $7,500 then the project will breakeven.

The PV of the labour costs using annuity factors is 25,000 × 3.784 = 94,600

Therefore 7,500/94,600 =   **7.93%**

185 A, D and E

Sensitivity analysis considers how far a variable needs to change before the decision would change but does not look at the probability of such a change. It is not an optimising technique – it provides information on the basis of which decisions can be made but does not point directly to the correct decision. By finding the extent by which each variable would need to change, sensitivity analysis identifies those flows which are most vulnerable and therefore crucial to the success of the project. Information will be presented to management in a form which facilitates subjective judgement to decide the likelihood of the various possible outcomes considered.

186 D

Sensitivity analysis can only show the impact of a cash flow changing, but not the likelihood.

187 B

Expected annual cash flow : 30 × 0.3 + 35 × 0.5 + 45 × 0.2 = $35.5 × 10,000 units = $355,000

Present value of $355,000 per annum – use 12% annuity factor of 3.605

$355,000 × 3.605 = $1,279,775

If you chose A you didn't round as the question asked. If you chose C, you used a discount factor not an annuity factor. If you chose D, you just calculated the single year cash flow and didn't discount.

188 $8,834

Cash flows	Probability	Year 1	Year 2
Optimistic	0.3 × 70,000	= 21,000	
	0.3 × 85,000		= 25,500
Most likely	0.45 × 40,000	= 18,000	
	0.45 × 55,000		= 24,750
Pessimistic	0.25 × 25,000	= 6,250	
	0.25 × 30,000		= 7,500
Total flow		**$45,250**	**$57,750**

NPV

Time	Cash flow	Discount factor	Present value
0	(80,000)	1	(80,000)
1	45,250	0.909	41,132
2	57,750	0.826	47,702
NPV			**$8,834**

189   A

Contribution at today's prices = 4,000 × $5 = $20,000. This increases by 3% per annum.

Year	Money cash	Discount at 8%	Present value
0	$(50,000)		$(50,000)
1	$20,600	0.926	$19,076
2	$21,218	0.857	$18,184
3	$21,855	0.794	$17,353
			$4,613

190   C

Inflation is now 4%. Continuing to work in money cash:

Year	Money cash	Try 14%	Present value
0	$(50,000)		$(50,000)
1	$20,800	0.877	$18,242
2	$21,632	0.769	$16,635
3	$22,497	0.675	$15,185
			$62

An NPV of $62 is virtually zero. Discounting at 14.5% would reduce the NPV by several hundred pounds. Therefore, the maximum monetary cost for the project to remain viable is 14%.

191   A

Annual contribution   = annual cash profit + annual cash fixed costs

                            = $450,000 + $190,000   = $640,000

Contribution/unit   = $220 – $55 = $165

∴ Units sold pa   = $640,000 ÷ $165   = 3,879 units.

The NPV of the project can fall by $127,600 before it becomes zero.

The NPV of total annual revenue is expected to be 3,879 × $220 × 4.623 = $3,945,175.

For this to fall by $127,600, it must suffer a decrease of $\dfrac{127,600}{3,945,175} \times 100\% = 3.2\%$

192 A

The present value of expected sales revenue is as follows:

Year	Item	Cash flow	Discount factor at 10%	PV
		$		$
1	Sales revenue	40,000	0.909	36,360
2	Sales revenue	40,000	0.826	33,040
3	Sales revenue	24,000	0.751	18,024
NPV				87,424

The NPV is $3,190, so the maximum reduction in sales price that can occur without the project ceasing to be viable is (3,190/87,424) = 0.036 = 3.6%.

193 B

The present value of the annual net cash flows, ignoring the machine cost and residual value, is: $(19,998 + 18,172 + 7,510) = $45,680.

If the machine costs $X, the net cost of the machine, in present value terms and allowing for the residual value at the end of year 3, is:

$X - (0.751 \times 20\% \text{ of } X)$

$= X - 0.1502X$

$= 0.8498X.$

If 0.8498X exceeds $45,680, the project will not be viable. The maximum amount the machine can cost without the project ceasing to be viable is therefore $45,680/0.8498 = $53,754, say $54,000.

194 E

Depreciation is included in investment appraisal where the company uses ARR as it is needed to calculate average annual profits. However it should never be included in discounted cash flow calculations as it is an accounting adjustment not a cash flow.

195 A

Quarterly tax payments are the standard assumption made about corporation tax – leading to its treatment as paid half in the year it arises and half in the following year. If assets are sold at a lower or higher price than the written down value this leads to a balancing allowance or a balancing charge. If they are sold at written down value no adjustment is needed. If investments are made over a two year period, the payments made within each year will be treated as paid on the last day of that year. However if the company is not making taxable profits, taxable losses on individual projects cannot be offset against future payments and the company will not be able to benefit from tax depreciation – both assumptions of standard NPV appraisal.

196 B

Relevant costs are future incremental cash flows (whether fixed or variable costs). The rent charge is not a cash flow but, in theory, it could represent a relevant opportunity cost – the value of the benefit sacrificed (the rent that would otherwise be earned from the space) when one course of action is chosen in preference to another. However, the cost here is a potential loss of rent only – i.e. it is a notional cost – but it is not an opportunity cost because no there is no identified opportunity to earn rent and no actual rent has been foregone.

197 C

Sensitivity = NPV of project/PV of figures which vary = $320,000/$630,000 = 51%

198

Year	Cash $	15%	PV $
0	(75,000)		(75,000)
1 – 5	25,000	3.352	83,800
			8,800

Try 20%

Year	Cash $	20%	PV $
0	(75,000)		(75,000)
1 – 5	25,000	2.991	74,775
			(225)

$$\text{IRR} = 15\% + \frac{8,800}{(8,800+225)} \times 5\%$$

$$\text{IRR} = 15\% + \frac{8,800}{9,025} \times 5\%$$

$$\text{IRR} = 19.88\%$$

PV of labour cost	=	$20,000 × 3.352
	=	$67,040

$$\therefore \text{Allowable change} = \frac{8,800}{67,040} \times 100$$

$$= 13.13\%$$

199 7.8%

Year	Discount factor	Increase in cost ($000)	Present value ($000)	Savings ($000)	Present value ($000)
1	0.833	16	13.328	150	124.95
2	0.694	20	13.880	160	111.04
3	0.579	24	13.896	170	98.43
4	0.482	30	14.460	180	86.76
			55.564		421.18

The Present Value of costs increases by $55,564; this means that NPV falls to $22,900 − $55,564 = − $32,664. Therefore, the present value of savings must rise by $32,664, or $\frac{32,664}{421,180} \times 100 = 7.8\%$.

200 C series for the pessimistic buyer; A series for the optimistic buyer, as the best possible result comes from getting a 'grade A' truck. C series for the buyer prone to regretting decisions (see regret table below) and C series for the risk neutral buyer, based on Expected Values calculations (see below.)

Regret table		Type of truck		
		A grade	B grade	C grade
Growth rate	15%	1,200	1,800	0
	30%	3,100	2,600	0
	40%	0	2,100	1,000
Max regret		3,100	2,600	1,000

Expected value calculations:

A Grade: $(2,400 \times 0.4) + (1,400 \times 0.25) + (4,900 \times 0.35) = 3,025$

B Grade: $(1,800 \times 0.4) + (1,900 \times 0.25) + (2,800 \times 0.35) = 2,175$

C Grade: $(3,600 \times 0.4) + (4,500 \times 0.25) + (3,900 \times 0.35) = 3,930$

201 A

The Monte Carlo simulation method uses random numbers and probability statistics to show the effect of more than one variable changing at the same time. It can be used to give management a view of the likely range and level of outcomes for a project.

The modified internal rate of return (MIRR) finds the expected economic yield of the investment. Capital rationing is used to find the project ranking which will maximise the company's NPV per $1 invested.

Expected profits are used to calculate the value of perfect information.

202   The third point did not apply. The following do apply:

○   Simulation models the behaviour of a system.

○   Simulation models can be used to study alternative solutions to a problem.

○   A simulation model cannot prescribe what should be done about a problem.

203 B

Without information, the expected profits are:

Product X: $\$20,000 \times 0.2 + \$15,000 \times 0.5 + \$6,000 \times 0.3$ = $\$13,300$

Product Y: $\$17,000 \times 0.2 + \$16,000 \times 0.5 + \$7,000 \times 0.3$ = $\$13,500$

So without information, product Y would be selected.

With perfect information, product X would be selected if the market was good, and product Y in the other two cases. The expected value would then be:

$\$20,000 \times 0.2 + \$16,000 \times 0.5 + \$7,000 \times 0.3$ = $\$14,100$

The expected value of perfect information is therefore $\$14,100 - \$13,500 = \$600$

204

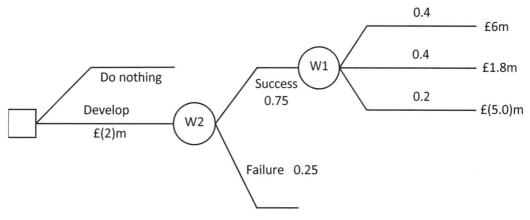

(W1) EV = $\$6m \times 0.4 + \$1.8m \times 0.4 - \$5m \times 0.2$

= $\$2.12m$

(W2) EV = $\$2.12m \times 0.75 + \$0 \times 0.25$

= $\$1.59m$

Net benefit: $\$1.59m - \$2m$

= $(\$0.41)m$

205   A

Additional sales 60 boxes × ($3 selling price − $2 cost)	$60
And unsold 40 boxes × ($1 selling price − $2 cost)	$(40)
Profit	$20
Probability	× 0.6
Expected value	$12
Additional sales 100 boxes × ($3 selling price − $2 cost)	$100
And unsold 0 boxes × ($1 selling price)	$0
Profit	$100
Probability	× 0.4
Expected profit	$40
Expected profit (value) of decision	**$52**

206   A

Most probability problems have you compute the expected value from a series of possible outcomes, each weighted with its own likelihood of occurrence. However, in this problem, the company only wants to select the most likely sales volume figure. That would be the one with the greatest probability of occurrence.

207   A

Selling price	x	Probability of selling price	=	Expected value
$5,000		40%		$2,000
$8,000		20%		$1,600
$12,000		30%		$3,600
$30,000		10%		$3,000
Expected selling price			=	**$10,200**

208   A

The probability of the lead time being 3 days is 25%, and the probability of demand being 3 units in a day is 10%. The probability of 3 days of demand being 3 units (3 × 3 = 9) coupled with a 3-day lead time is as follows: 0.25 × 0.1 × 0.1 × 0.1 = 0.00025

209   E

Forecast	Actual sales		
	High	Low	
High	0.5525	0.0525	0.605
Low	0.0975	0.2975	0.395
	0.65	0.35	1.00

Probability = 0.0975/0.395 = 0.2468

210 Using 1,000 as a suitable multiple, i.e. considering 1,000 cakes are baked, the contingency table is:

	Made at factory		
	X	Y	Total
Has not been baked properly	30	84	114
Has been baked properly	270	616	886
Total	300	700	1,000

Therefore, P (Made in bakery B/not baked properly) = 84/114 = 0.737 or 73.7%

211 RECYC

Payoff table

		Level of waste		
		High	Medium	Low
Advance	High	962.5	636.5	397.5
order of	Medium	912.5	655.5	442.5
chemical	Low	837.5	617.5	457.5

(W1)

Advance order of chemical X	Level of waste	Prob.	Contrib. (excl. X) (W2) $000	Chemical X cost (W3) $000	Net contribution $000
High	High	0.30	1,462.5	500	962.5
	Medium	0.50	1,111.5	475	636.5
	Low	0.20	877.5	480	397.5
Medium	High	0.30	1,462.5	550	912.5
	Medium	0.50	1,111.5	456	655.5
	Low	0.20	877.5	435	442.5
Low	High	0.30	1,462.5	625	837.5
	Medium	0.50	1,111.5	494	617.5
	Low	0.20	877.5	420	457.5

(W2) Waste available

	High	Medium	Low
Aluminium extracted (000 kg)	7,500	5,700	˙4,500
	$000	$000	$000
Sales revenue (at $0.65 per kg)	4,875.0	3,705.0	2,925.0
Variable cost (at 70%)	3,412.5	2,593.5	2,047.5
Contribution	1,462.5	1,111.5	877.5

Maximax suggests that the decision maker should look for the largest possible profit from all the outcomes. In this case this is a high advance order of chemical X where there is a possibility of a contribution of $962,500. This indicates a risk seeking preference by management. Although it offers the possibility of the highest contribution, there is also a 20% likelihood that the worst outcome of $397,500 will occur.

Maximin suggests that the decision maker should look for the strategy which maximises the minimum possible contribution. In this case this is a low advance order of chemical X where the lowest contribution is $457,500. This is better than the worst possible outcomes from high or medium advance orders of chemical X. This indicates a risk-averse management posture.

(W3) Examples of workings for chemical X cost

- High advance level of order for chemical X and low actual requirement: The price of $1.00 is subject to a penalty of $0.60 per kg. The cost of chemical X is, therefore, 300,000 kg × $1.60 = $480,000

- Low advance level of order for chemical X and medium actual requirement: The price is subject to a discount of $0.10 per kg. The cost of chemical X is, therefore, 380,000 × $1.30 = $494,000.

212 TICKET AGENT

(a)   The question specifies that a long-run perspective is being taken so decisions can be made by reference to expected values.

Expected sales demand

	Probability	Demand	EV
Popular artistes	0.45	500	225
Lesser known artistes	0.30	350	105
Unknown artistes	0.25	200	50
			380

Expected demand = 380 tickets per concert

Maximising profit

To determine the best decision, the expected profits for each possible order level need to be calculated.

- Payoff table showing profit (W1, W2)

		Actual sales demand		
		200	350	500
	200	1,200	1,200	1,200
Purchase	300	(570)	2,250	2,250
Level	400	(2,040)	2,190	3,600
	500	(2,460)	1,770	6,000

- Expected values

		EV
200 tickets	1,200 × 1	1,200
300 tickets	(570) × 0.25 + 2,250 × 0.75	1,545
400 tickets	(2,040) × 0.25 + 2,190 × 0.3 + 3,600 × 0.45	1,767
500 tickets	(2,460) × 0.25 + 1,770 × 0.3 + 6,000 × 0.45	2,616

The optimum purchase level is 500 tickets per concert, which will give an expected profit of $2,616 per concert.

Workings

(W1) The gross profit made per ticket is the discount received on the selling price of $30.

Purchase level	Discount			Profit per ticket sold
200	20%	20% × $30	=	$6.00
300	25%	25% × $30	=	$7.50
400	30%	30% × $30	=	$9.00
500	40%	40% × $30	=	$12.00

(W2) Each net profit calculation consists of up to three elements:

1   the profit on the units sold

2   the cost of the units which are unsold and returned

3   the value of the returns

EV of returns = $30.00 × 60% × 10% = $1.80 per return.

Example calculation:

Buy 300 tickets but can only sell 200 $\Rightarrow$ Sell 200 tickets and return 100 tickets

	$
Sales 200 tickets × 7.50 (W1)	1,500
EV of returns 100 tickets × $1.80	180
	1,680
Cost of returns 100 tickets × $22.50 (25% discount)	(2,250)
	(570)

(b) **Maximax**

The agent should order 500 tickets as this gives a maximum possible gain of $6,000 per concert.

Maximin

The agent should buy 200 tickets to maximise the minimum possible pay-off ($1,200).

Minimax regret

A regret table is found by comparing the actual profit with what could have been made given the level of demand that occurred:

		Actual sales demand		
		200	350	500
	200	0	1,050	4,800
Purchase	300	1,770	0	3,750
Level	400	3,240	60	2,400
	500	3,660	480	0

The agent would thus order 400 tickets as this limits the maximum regret to $3,240.

This level of order would give an average profit of $1,767 per concert.

213 SHIFTERS HAULAGE

Profit calculations

	Small van	Medium van	Large van
Capacity	100	150	200
Low Demand (120)	300 (W1)	468 (W3)	368 (W5)
High Demand (190)	300 (W2)	500 (W4)	816 (W6)

Workings	(W1)	(W2)	(W3)	(W4)	(W5)	(W6)
Sales	1,000	1,000	1,200	1,500	1,200	1,900
VC	(400)	(400)	(480)	(600)	(480)	(760)
Goodwill	(100)	(100)		(100)		
VC adjustment			48		48	76
Depreciation	(200)	(200)	(300)	(300)	(400)	(400)
Profit	300	300	468	500	368	816

214 COOL SYSTEMS

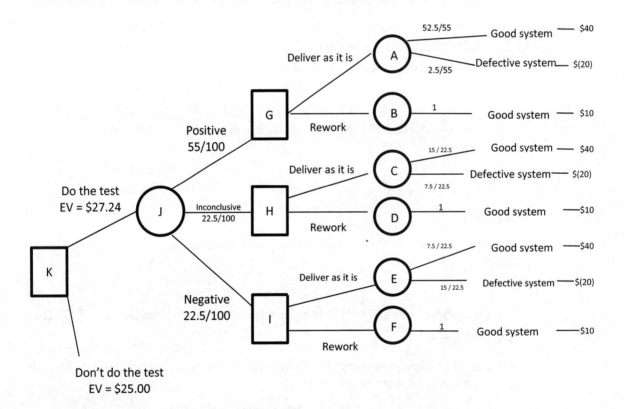

EV(A) = [(52.5/55) × $40)] − [(2.5/55)X $20)] = $37.27

EV(B) = $10

So our choice at 'G' will be to **deliver the system as it is**.

EV(C) = [(15/22.5) × $40)] − [(7.5/22.5)X $20)] = $20

EV(D) = $10

So our choice at 'H' will be to **deliver the system as it is**.

EV(E) = [(7.5/22.5) × $40)] − [(15/22.5)X $20)] = $0

EV(F) = $10

So our choice at 'I' will be to **rework the system**.

EV(J) = (0.55 × $37.27) + (0.225 × $20) + (0.225 × $10) = $27.24

Therefore EV of Imperfect Information: $27.24 − $25.00 = $2.24

215 THEATRE

Ticket sales ($)	Confectionary sales ($)	Total sales ($)	Joint × probability	Sales × probability ($)
7,500	900	8,400	.5 × .3 = .15	1,260
7,500	1,500	9,000	.5 × .5 = .25	2,250
7,500	3,000	10,500	.5 × .2 = .10	1,050
10,000	1,200	11,200	.3 × .3 = .09	1,008
10,000	2,000	12,000	.3 × .5 = .15	1,800
10,000	4,000	14,000	.3 × .2 = .06	840
12,500	1,500	14,000	.2 × .3 = .06	840
12,500	2,500	15,000	.2 × .5 = .10	1,500
12,500	5,000	17,500	.2 × .2 = .04	700
Total			1.00	11,248

The expected value is $11,248 − $10,000 = $1,248. Therefore it is worthwhile engaging MS for the concert.

The data table shows profit values from each combination of ticket sales and contribution from confectionary sales. So, for example, for 300 people and $3 per person total sales are $8,400 (from (a)) − $10,000 fee = $1,600 loss.

Confectionary sales / Ticket sales	$3 per person	$5 per person	$10 per person
300 people	(1,600)	(1,000)	500
400 people	1,200	2,000	4,000
500 people	4,000	5,000	7,500

216 AMELIE

In order to decide whether or not to hire the consultant, expected valued for decision alternatives are calculated, starting on the right hand side of the tree and moving leftwards (backtracking).

At node D:

EV(I) = (0.9 × $30,000) − (0.1 × $10,000) = $26,000

EV(J) = (0.9 × $60,000) − (0.1 × $40,000) = $50,000

EV(K) = (0.9 × $0) − (0.1 × $0) = $0

So, the decision at Node D should be to go for a large shop, as the EV of outcome J is the highest of the three possible decisions I, J and K.

At node E:

EV(L) = (0.12 × $30,000) – (0.88 × $10,000) = ($5,200)

EV(M) = (0.12 × $60,000) – (0.88 × $40,000) = ($28,000)

EV(N) = (0.12 × $0) – (0.88 × $0) = $0

So, the decision at Node E should be not to go for any shop at all, as the EV of outcome N is the only non-loss making option.

At node C:

EV(F) = (0 .5 × $30,000) – (0.5 × $10,000) = $10,000

EV(G) = (0.5 × $60,000) – (0.5 × $40,000) = $10,000

EV(H) = (0.5 × $0) – (0.5 × $0) = $0

So, the decision at Node C should be to go for either a small or a large shop, as both offer the same positive EV of a profit.

To decide between hiring a consultant at $5,000 and not hiring a consultant, we need to calculate the EV of profits at node B:

EV (B) = (0.6 × $50,000) + (0.4 × $0) = $30,000

Therefore, profits if a consultant is hired are expected to reach

$30,000 – cost of research $5,000 = $25,000

EV (C) = $10,000, if no market research is undertaken. The expected value of profits is higher if market research is undertaken, therefore Amelie should hire the consultant.

- We first need to calculate what the expected value of profits with perfect information would be. If the second consultant predicts a favourable cheese market (0.6 probability), we should opt for a large shop and obtain $60,000 profit. If the consultant predicts an unfavourable market, we should not go for no shop at all (and profits will be nil.)

Therefore EV of profits with perfect information	= 0.6 × $60,000 + (0 × $0)
	= $36,000
Expected profit with imperfect market research information from first consultant	
	= $25,000
Value of perfect information	= $11,000

217 C

Decision trees incorporate expected values and do not generate perfect information relating to a sequence of decisions and outcomes.

218 C

Valorisation

219 Big Data management involves using sophisticated <u>systems</u> to <u>gather</u>, store and <u>analyse</u> large volumes of data in a variety of <u>structured</u> and <u>unstructured</u> formats. In addition to <u>traditional</u> data from internal sources such as sales history, preferences, order frequency and pricing information, companies can also gather information from <u>external</u> sources such as <u>websites</u>, trade publications and <u>social networks</u>.

Collating and analysing these large volumes of information allows companies to gain a variety of <u>insights</u> into customer behaviour and this can help to more accurately predict <u>customer demand</u>.

These demand forecasts may be in terms of volume but also the type of products required and this is beneficial to company <u>planning</u> but can also help the company to improve aspects of the <u>customer experience</u>. In terms of volume predictions, these can help to ensure that a company will always have sufficient inventory to satisfy demand. This will mean that customers do not need to wait to receive their goods which is likely to be a key part of their shopping experience. Furthermore companies can use the information and <u>insights</u> to understand which products and <u>features</u> are most popular with customers. This can inform product re-design to ensure that any revisions are in line with customer preferences.

220 Business data can be difficult to manage for a variety of reasons and these can be summarised using the 3 V's of velocity, volume and variety.

Velocity

The speed at which data is now generated from sources such as social media networks makes it incredibly difficult for <u>traditional</u> database management systems to cope and give relevant and timely <u>insights</u>. If this <u>data</u> is not managed effectively it is, at best, <u>wasted</u> but could also result in significant increases in the data <u>storage</u> capacity required, without seeing any particular benefits.

Volume

Companies can now gather and generate data from a huge range of <u>sources</u> including internal systems, <u>e-commerce</u> sources, competitor and customer websites and social media networks. Not only has the overall <u>volume</u> of sources increased but the amount of data gathered from each source is now much higher than from <u>traditional</u> reporting. For example the data gathered from a single e-commerce sales transaction can be up to ten times higher than a <u>standard</u> in-store transaction. It is important that data is only gathered (and therefore stored and analysed) from relevant <u>sources</u> that can actually add value to company decision making as there is a danger that companies become obsessed with gathering all data that is available rather than just that which is <u>useful</u>.

Variety

An increasing number of incompatible and inconsistent data formats is emerging at a fast rate. Most traditional data management <u>systems</u> are based around extracting data from, and storing data in, standard formats such as XML. Collecting data in a wide variety of formats including sound files and GPS data creates challenges for a system managing such big data.

221 A

222 B

223 D

224 C

225 B

The following information is given by the question:

(i)   There are 100 students in total.

(ii)   30 students are male (hence 100 – 30 = 70 are female).

(iii)   55 students are studying for Certificate Stage (hence 100 – 55 = 45 are not studying for Certificate Stage).

(iv)   6 male students are not studying (hence 30 – 6 = 24 are studying).

For simplicity this information can be placed into a table.

	Not studying	Studying	Total
Male	6	(30 – 6) = 24	30
Female	(45 – 6) = 39	(70 – 39) = 31	70
Total	45	55	100

The probability that a randomly chosen female student is not studying is $\frac{39}{70}$,

i.e. P(NS/F) = 0.56.

226 The probability that a randomly-selected Brand X buyer is from the north and under 25 years of age is (to 2 decimal places):

P =	**0.08**

The probability that a randomly-selected Brand X buyer is from the West or under 25 years of age is (to 2 decimal places):

P =	**0.48**

The probability that a randomly-selected Brand X buyer, who is under 25 years of age, is from the South is (to 3 decimal places):

P =	**0.375**

The probability that two randomly-selected Brand X buyers are both under 25 years of age is (to two decimal places):

P =	**0.09**

Workings

(i)   Probability = 400/5,200 = 0.769 = 0.08

(ii)   West buyers   = 1,300

Under 25s   = 1,600

West and under 25   = 400

West or under 25   = 1,300 + 1,600 − 400

                         = 2,500

Probability   = 2,500/5,200

                         = 0.48

(iii)   Probability   = 600/1,600 = 0.375

(iv)   Probability   = 1,600/5,200 × 1,599/5,199 = 0.0946 = 0.09